BASIC COMPUTERS FOR SENIORS AND BEGINNERS

by

Dr Alfonso J. Kinglow

Printed in the United States of America

Library of Congress Control Number: 12345678

DEDICATION

I would like to Dedicate this book to my wife Sarah for all of her Love, Care and Support and to my daughters Sarah, Keren and Karina, my Strength, My Light, and my Joy. You have made me a proud Father and a better man. I love you, and all of my Grandchildren

INDEX

ACKNOWLEDGMENTS

I would like to thank Phillip Moreno and all of his Staff, and Alex Ruiz, of Shadow Mountain Senior Center in Phoenix Arizona for all of their support and help in setting up my Computer Classes for the Seniors and for their support in providing a location for the Classes; Thank you. And For all the great work they do for our Seniors in Phoenix, Arizona. Thank you Alex for your continued support.
Thank You.

1 CHAPTER ONE
WHAT IS A COMPUTER

A Computer consist of Hardware and Software. The Hardware contains the Memory, Storage and CPU, the Mouse and Keyboard and the Video Display with many internal parts like the Network Adapter and the Video Graphics Card and DVD player.

The Software is the program that runs the Computer Hardware, it is called the System Software or the Operating System. In this case the Operating System is a **GUI** (Graphic User Interface) type called **Windows.**

The other many Software that runs on the Computer are called: Applications,Utilities, Programs, Diagnostics, Administrative, System, User Programs, and Tools.

Computers are Digital Machines and use their own Computer Language called Binary Language, that represents (0) zero and (1) one.
Computers began in the Analog World and we can say Computers are divided into Digital and Analog.

Analog Computers needed a Cable to communicate between computers, by sending a Signal (Sound Wave) or **Sine Wave.** If the Cable was too long, then the Signal would Degrade. Coaxial Cable was used to preserve the Signal, and two Cables were used. The Transmit Cable and the Receive Cable. Zero (0) Decibels or Zero db. At 600 Ohms Termination, was used as a Standard for Testing and

Transmitting and Receiving a signal. The zero Decibel Signal was generated by an Electronic Device called an Oscillator produced by a Vacuum Tube called a TRIODE that consisted of a Plate, Grid and Filaments.

Somewhere after 1965 aprox. The Digital Signal was discovered and Developed by IBM, SPARK, Xerox, DEC and others., and the Digital Era began.

An IC or Integrated Circuit Chip was built called an A/D and a D/A Chip. Analog to Digital and Digital to Analog Converters. An Analog Signal could then be converted to Digital Form using 0 zero and one (1) and a **Square Wave** was born.

The **Square Wave** is a Binary Signal that starts from **zero** then rises to **1 volt,** with a time of **1 sec** then dropping to **zero** again., a Binary number is then created, or 010. This Binary number is called a **BIT,** and represents zero (0) or one (1), OFF/ON. Therefore; the smallest Unit of Information that can be Transmitted is a **BIT.**

Computers using zero's and one's to communicate, or bits per second (bps) form a BINARY LANGUAGE, used by Computers all over the World.

Because the **BIT** is very small, it was organized into more larger and manageable sizes that would handle the large and vast requirements for **Storage and Memory,** so STANDARDS had to be created.
The Standard for **MEMORY** begins with 1 Gb, then 2-4-8-16-32-64-128-256-512-**1024 Gb**. (Giga-Bytes)etc..

Computers with 3 and 6 Gigabytes are not recommended; as Memory works in Equal Pairs. Eight Gigabytes (8 Gb.)

should be **4Gb + 4Gb = 8 Gb.**
  The Beginning.__ IBM – XEROX – SPARK – DEC.

IBM first PC, The IBM Pcjr also called The Rainbow Computer, was the result of the Digital Era.

THE ANALOG WORLD. ____

A) The ANALOG Wave is a SINE WAVE or Audio Signal that is SINO SUOIDAL or Low sound to high sound back to low sound.. Going from 0 (zero) signal to One (1) High Signal., measured in CYCLES PER SECOND., (CPS); also called HERTZ, Hz. Named after Heinrich Hertz (German Physicist) who discovered it.

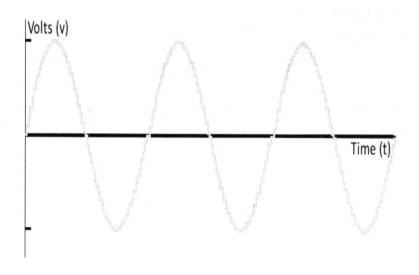

Volts (v)

Time (t)

The SPEED of the Signal is Measured in Hz. Or Cycles - per-Second

(cps). The Computer (CPU) Central Processing Unit, is measured in Giga-hertz or Ghz. Example:

Intel CPU 2.5 Ghz. Is the Speed of the Processor.

THE DIGITAL WORLD. _____

The **Smallest unit** of Information that can be transmitted is a **BIT**. A **BIT** is a Binary Number that Represents (0) **ZERO** or One (1). The BINARY Language is used by all Computers to communicate and is called The Computer Language. The BIT uses a **Voltage Signal** that starts from 0 (zero) and rises to 1 (one) for 1 second, then drops to Zero (0) representing **ON**/1 and **OFF**/0. **<u>Welcome to the Digital World.</u>**

<u>16 Bits is equal to:</u> **1 BYTE**

A KILO-BYTE is equal to: 1024 BYTE'S

A MEGA-BYTE is equal to: 1024 KILO-BYTE'S

A GIGA-BYTE is equal to: 1024 MEGA-BYTE'S

Kilo, Mega and Giga = Greek designators in Binary Numbers.

One KILO- METER = 1000 Meters

Difference Between MB and GB. The rate of **data** transmission in telecommunications and computer use is based on the number of bits, characters, or blocks in their systems. ... Today a byte consists of 16 bits, a kilobyte is 1024 bytes, a megabyte is 1024 kilobytes, and a **gigabyte** is 1024 megabytes.

KB, **MB**, **GB** - A kilobyte (KB) is 1,024 bytes. A megabyte (**MB**) is 1,024 kilobytes. A gigabyte (**GB**) is 1,024 megabytes. A terabyte (TB) is 1,024 gigabytes.

A bit can be 0 or 1, equivalent or off or on. ... Therefore 1KB is the same as 1024 x 8 = 8192 binary digits. Megabyte (**MB**): 1024KB equals one megabyte (**MB**). Gigabyte (**GB**): There are 1024MB in one gigabyte.

Maximum Data Transmission in Computers.

Kilobyte (1024 Bytes)

Megabyte (1024 Kilobytes)

Gigabyte (1,024 Megabytes, or 1,048,576 Kilobytes)

Terabyte (1,024 Gigabytes)

Petabyte (1,024 Terabytes, or 1,048,576 Gigabytes)

Exabyte (1,024 Petabytes)

Zettabyte (1,024 Exabytes)

Yottabyte (1,204 Zettabytes,

or 1,208,925,819,614,629,174,706,176 bytes)

History and origin of kilo, mega and more.

The prefix *kilo* (1,000) first came into existence between 1865 and 1870. Though *mega* is used these days to mean "extremely good, great or successful," its scientific meaning is 1 million.

Giga **comes from the Greek** word for giant, and the first use of the term is believed to have taken place at the 1947 conference of the International Union of Pure and Applied Chemistry. *Tera* (1 trillion) **comes from the Greek** word *teras* or *teratos,* meaning "marvel, monster," and has been in use since approximately 1947.

The prefixes *exa* (1 quintillion) and *peta* (1 quadrillion) were added to the <u>International System of Units</u> (<u>SI</u>) in 1975. However, the origin and history of *peta* with data measurement terms is unclear. *Zetta* (1 sextillion) was added to the SI metric prefixes in 1991.

When the prefixes are added to the term *byte,* it creates units of measurement ranging from **1,000 bytes (kilobyte) to 1 sextillion bytes (<u>zettabyte</u>)** of <u>data storage capacity.</u> **A megabyte is 1 million bytes of data storage capacity, according to the IBM Dictionary of Computing.**

A gigabyte (<u>GB</u>) is equivalent to about **1 billion bytes.** There are two standards for measuring the number of bytes in a gigabyte: base-10 and base-2. Base-10 uses the decimal system to show that 1 GB equals one to the 10th power of bytes, or 1 billion bytes. <u>This is the standard most data storage manufacturers and consumers use today.</u> Computers typically use the base-2, or binary, form of measurement. Base-2 has 1 GB as equal to 1,073,741,824 bytes. The discrepancy between base-10 and base-2 measurements became more distinct as vendors began to manufacture data storage media with more capacity.

A terabyte (TB) is equal to approximately **1 trillion bytes,** or 1,024 GB. **A petabyte** (PB) is equal to two to the 50th power of bytes. There are **1,024 TB in a PB,** and about **1,024 PB equal 1 exabyte (EB).** A **zettabyte** is equal to about 1,000 EB, or **1 billion TB.**

Terabyte vs. petabyte: What would it look like?

In his book, *The Singularity is Near*, futurist Raymond Kurzweil estimated **the capacity of a human being's functional memory to be 1.25 TB.** This means that the memories of 800 human beings fit into 1 PB of storage.

If the average MP3 encoding is approximately 1 MB per second (MBps), and the average song lasts about **four minutes,** then a petabyte of songs could play continuously for more than 2,000 years.

If the average smartphone camera photo is 3 MB, and the average printed photo is 8.5-inches wide, a petabyte of photos placed side by side would be more than **48,000 miles long.**

That is almost long enough to wrap around the equator twice. According to Wes Biggs, CTO at

Adfonic, **1 PB can store the DNA of the entire population of the United States and then clone them twice.**

If you counted all the bits in 1 PB of storage at a rate of 1 bps, it would take **285 million years,** according to data analysts from Deloitte Analytics.

A bit is a binary digit, either a 0 or 1; a byte is eight binary digits long. If you counted 1 bps, it would take 35.7 million years.

Yottabytes and Data Storage

The future of data storage may be the **yottabyte.** It's a measure of Storage capacity equal to approximately 1,000 zettabytes, 1 trillion terabytes, a million trillion megabytes or 1 septillion bytes.

Written in decimal form, a yottabyte looks like this: 1,208,925,819,614,629,174,706,176. The prefix *yotta* is based on the

Greek letter iota. According to Paul McFedries' book *Word Spy*, it **would take 86 trillion years to download a 1 yottabyte file;** by comparison, the entire contents of the Library of Congress would equal just 10 TB.

According to a 2010 Gizmodo article, storing a yottabyte of data on terabyte-size disk drives would require 1 billion city block-size data centers, equal to combining the states of Rhode Island and Delaware.

As of late 2016, memory density had grown to the point where a yottabyte could be stored on <u>SDX cards</u> occupying no more than twice the size of the Hindenberg.

Digital Signal. __

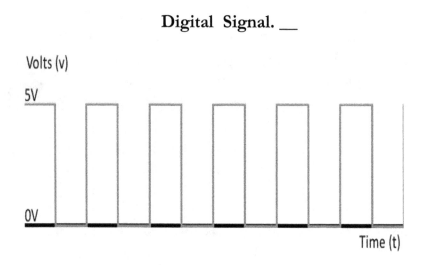

2 CHAPTER TWO
COMPUTER HARDWARE AND SOFTWARE

Computer Hardware and Software. **The Hardware** contains the Memory, Storage and CPU, the Mouse and

Keyboard and the Video Display with many internal parts like the Network Adapter and the Video Graphics Card and DVD player.

The Software is the program that runs the Computer Hardware, it is called the System Software or the Operating System. In this case the Operating System is a **GUI** (Graphic User Interface) type, called **Windows.**

USING EXPLORER SHELL AND COMMANDS. _

TO CREATE A PORTABLE FOLDER OF ANY PART OF WINDOWS SYSTEM.__

USING **" EXPLORER SHELL"**

Create a Short Cut Folder by selecting NEW and **Shortcut**

In the **Shortcut** window: **Type: Explorer Shell:** and the name of the Part of

Windows you want to create: <u>for Example:</u>

      Explorer Shell:ControlPanelFolder   and click NEXT

      another window will be displayed.

      Type the name you want to give to the folder, and press <Finish>

      The new folder will be created.

<u>Another Example</u>: **Explorer Shell:AppsFolder The All Applications Folder will be Created.**

1. This folder will be portable and can be used on any Windows Computer.

First you'll need to create a new shortcut. To do this, right-click on Desktop and select **"New -> Shortcut"**: then type explorer shell: and type the name of the tool you want to create: IE: **Explorer shell:ControlPanelFolder**

CREATING A RESTORE POINT IN WINDOWS. __

The Purpose of Creating a Restore Point in Windows.

It is so important to create a Restore Point in Windows to avoid loosing all of your work.
And many times the Computer might freeze up caused by a virus or some other problem, and the user may not be able to get to his files or access Windows.

Restoring all of the user files from a " Known good date" is critical and will save the day.

Follow the instructions on the next page to setup and create a <u>RESTORE POINT.</u>

Enable System Protection / Create a Restore Point

What happens if you install a bad piece of software or a defective driver and your computer starts acting strangely or you can't even boot. You'll want to revert Windows 10 to the previous system restore point, which will turn back the clock on your drivers, programs and settings to a time when the system worked perfectly. However, Windows 10 comes with system protection disabled. If you want to protect yourself -- and you should -- set up restore points following the instructions below.

1. Search for "restore point" in the Windows search box.

2. Launch "Create a restore point" from the results. You should see a list of available drives.

3. Select the system drive and click Configure. The system drive is usually the C: drive and has the word "(System)" written after its volume name.

4. Toggle Restore Settings to "Turn on system protection," set the maximum disk space usage by moving the slider and click Ok. We recommend

leaving 2 or 3 percent for restore pints but you may be able to get away with the lowest (1 percent).

5. Click Create so that you create an initial restore point right away.

6. Name the initial restore point when prompted.

7. Click Close when it is done.

If you need to restore from one of these points, you can click the System Restore button on the System Protection tab. If you can't boot, you can hit F8 or Shift + F8 during boot to get to the emergency menu on some computers. On other PCs, if you can at least get to the log in screen, you can hold down Shift while you select Restart.

INTERNET DEFINITIONS. _

Internet

An international conglomeration of interconnected computer networks. Begun in the late 1960s, it was developed in the 1970s to allow government and university researchers to share information. The Internet is not controlled by any single group or organization. Its original focus was research and communications, but it continues to expand, offering a wide array of resources for business and home users.

IP (Internet Protocol) address

An Internet Protocol address is a unique set of numbers used to locate another computer on a network. The format of an IP address is a 32-bit string of four numbers separated by periods. Each number can be from 0 to 255 (i.e., 1.154.10.255). Within a closed network IP addresses may be assigned at random, however, IP addresses of Web Servers must be registered to avoid duplicates.

COMPUTER SOFTWARE.__

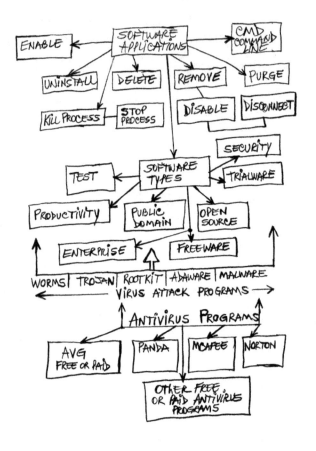

WORMS | TROJAN | ROOTKIT | ADAWARE | MALWARE
VIRUS ATTACK PROGRAMS →

ANTIVIRUS PROGRAMS

2016 COPYRIGHT ©ALFONSO J. KINGLOW

Using Computer Software SHELL.__

WINDOWS SHELL COMMANDS. ____

You can use any of following Commands to create the desired shortcut:

explorer shell:MyComputerFolder (for My Computer shortcut)

explorer shell:RecycleBinFolder (for Recycle Bin shortcut)

explorer shell:ControlPanelFolder (for Control Panel shortcut)

explorer shell:Administrative Tools (for Administrative Tools shortcut)

explorer shell:ChangeRemoveProgramsFolder (for Programs and Features shortcut)

explorer shell:NetworkPlacesFolder (for Network shortcut)

explorer shell:Favorites (for Favorites shortcut)

explorer shell:HomegroupFolder (for Homegroup shortcut)

explorer shell:Games (for Games shortcut)

explorer shell:Fonts (for Fonts shortcut)

explorer shell:UserProfiles (for Users folder shortcut)

explorer shell:Profile (for your username folder shortcut)

explorer shell:Public (for Public folder shortcut)

explorer shell:My Documents (for Documents

shortcut)

explorer shell:Common Documents (for Public Documents shortcut)

explorer shell:My Music (for Music folder shortcut)

explorer shell:CommonMusic (for Public Music folder shortcut)

explorer shell:My Pictures (for Pictures folder shortcut)

explorer shell:CommonPictures (for Public Pictures folder shortcut)

explorer shell:My Video (for Videos folder shortcut)

explorer shell:CommonVideo (for Public Videos folder shortcut)

explorer shell:Downloads (for Downloads folder shortcut)

explorer shell:CommonDownloads (for Public Downloads folder shortcut)

explorer shell:::{3080F90E-D7AD-11D9-BD98-0000947B0257} (for Flip 3D or Window Switcher shortcut)

EXTENDED SHELL COMMANDS :

Shell Command	Description
shell:AccountPictures	Account Pictures
shell:AddNewProgramsFolder	The "Get Programs" Control panel item
shell:Administrative Tools	Administrative Tools

shell:AppData   Same as %appdata%, the
c:\user\<username>\appdata\roaming folder
shell:Application Shortcuts   Opens the folder which
stores all Modern apps shortcuts
shell:AppsFolder   The virtual folder which stores all
installed Modern apps
shell:AppUpdatesFolder   The "Installed Updates"
Control panel item
shell:Cache   IE's cache folder (Temporary
Internet Files)
shell:CD Burning   Temporary Burn Folder
shell:ChangeRemoveProgramsFolder   The "Uninstall a
program" Control panel item
shell:Common Administrative Tools   The Administrative
Tools folder for all users
shell:Common AppData   The C:\ProgramData
folder (%ProgramData%)
shell:Common Desktop   Public Desktop
shell:Common Documents   Public Documents
shell:Common Programs   All Users Programs,
which are part of Start menu. Still used by the Start screen
shell:Common Start Menu   All Users Start Menu
folder, same as above
shell:Common Startup   The Startup folder, used
for all users
shell:Common Templates   Same as above, but used
for new documents templates, e.g. by Microsoft Office
shell:CommonDownloads   Public Downloads
shell:CommonMusic   Public Music

shell:CommonPictures	Public Pictures
shell:CommonRingtones	Public Ringtones folder
shell:CommonVideo	Public Videos
shell:ConflictFolder	The Control Panel\All

Control Panel Items\Sync Center\Conflicts item

shell:ConnectionsFolder	The Control Panel\All

Control Panel Items\Network Connections item

shell:Contacts	Contacts folder (Address book)
shell:ControlPanelFolder	Control Panel
shell:Cookies	The folder with IE's cookies
shell:CredentialManager	

C:\Users\<username>\AppData\Roaming\Microsoft\Credentials

shell:CryptoKeys

C:\Users\<username>\AppData\Roaming\Microsoft\Crypto

shell:CSCFolder	This folder is broken in

Windows 8/7, provides access to the Offline files item

shell:Desktop	Desktop

shell:Device Metadata Store

C:\ProgramData\Microsoft\Windows\DeviceMetadataStore

shell:DocumentsLibrary	Documents Library
shell:Downloads	Downloads folder

shell:DpapiKeys

C:\Users\<username>\AppData\Roaming\Microsoft\Protect

shell:Favorites	Favorites
shell:Fonts	C:\Windows\Fonts

shell:Games   The Games Explorer item

shell:GameTasks

shell:HomeGroupFolder   The Home Group root
folder

shell:ImplicitAppShoC:\Users\<username>\AppData\Lo
cal\Microsoft\Windows\GameExplorer

shell:History
C:\Users\<username>\AppData\Local\Microsoft\Wind
ows\History, IE's browsing history

shell:HomeGroupCurrentUserFolder   The Home Group
folder for the current user

rtcuts
C:\Users\<username>\AppData\Roaming\Microsoft\Int
ernet Explorer\Quick Launch\User
Pinned\ImplicitAppShortcuts

shell:InternetFolder   This shell command will start
Internet Explorer

shell:Libraries   Libraries

shell:Links   The "Favorites" folder from the
Explorer navigation pane.

shell:Local AppData
C:\Users\<username>\AppData\Local

shell:LocalAppDataLow
C:\Users\<username>\AppData\LocalLow

shell:LocalizedResourcesDir   This shell folder is
broken in Windows 8

shell:MAPIFolder   Represents the Microsoft
Outlook folder

shell:MusicLibrary   Music Library

shell:My Music   The "My Music" folder (not the Library)

shell:My Pictures   The "My Pictures" folder (not the Library)

shell:My Video   The "My Videos" folder (not the Library)

shell:MyComputerFolder Computer/Drives view

shell:NetHood
C:\Users\<username>\AppData\Roaming\Microsoft\Windows\Network Shortcuts

shell:NetworkPlacesFolder The Network Places folder which shows computers and devices on your network

shell:OEM Links   This shell command does nothing on my Windows 8 Retail edition. Maybe it works with OEM Windows 8 editions.

shell:Original Images Not functional on Windows 8

shell:Personal   The "My Documents" folder (not the Library)

shell:PhotoAlbums   Saved slideshows, seems to have not been implemented yet

shell:PicturesLibrary Pictures Library

shell:Playlists   Stores WMP Playlists.

shell:PrintersFolder The classic "Printers" folder (not 'Devices and Printers')

shell:PrintHood
C:\Users\<username>\AppData\Roaming\Microsoft\Windows\Printer Shortcuts

shell:Profile   The User profile folder

shell:ProgramFiles   Program Files

shell:ProgramFilesCommon   C:\Program
Files\Common Files

shell:ProgramFilesCommonX86   C:\Program Files
(x86)\Common Files - for Windows x64

shell:ProgramFilesX86   C:\Program Files (x86) -
for Windows x64

shell:Programs
C:\Users\<username>\AppData\Roaming\Microsoft\Wi
ndows\Start Menu\Programs (Per-user Start Menu
Programs folder)

shell:Public   C:\Users\Public

shell:PublicAccountPictures
C:\Users\Public\AccountPictures

shell:PublicGameTasks
C:\ProgramData\Microsoft\Windows\GameExplorer

shell:PublicLibraries   C:\Users\Public\Libraries

shell:Quick Launch
C:\Users\<username>\AppData\Roaming\Microsoft\Int
ernet Explorer\Quick Launch

shell:Recent   The "Recent Items" folder
(Recent Documents)

shell:RecordedTVLibrary   The "Recorded TV"
Library

shell:RecycleBinFolder   Recycle Bin

shell:ResourceDir   C:\Windows\Resources
where visual styles are stored

shell:Ringtones

C:\Users\<username>\AppData\Local\Microsoft\Wind
ows\Ringtones

shell:Roamed Tile Images   Is not implemented yet.
Reserved for future.

shell:Roaming Tiles
C:\Users\<username>\AppData\Local\Microsoft\Wind
ows\RoamingTiles

shell:SavedGames   Saved Games

shell:Screenshots   The folder for Win+Print
Screen screenshots

shell:Searches   Saved Searches

shell:SearchHomeFolder   Windows Search UI

shell:SendTo   The folder with items that you
can see in the "Send to" menu

shell:Start Menu
C:\Users\<username>\AppData\Roaming\Microsoft\Wi
ndows\Start Menu (Per-user Start Menu folder)

shell:Startup   Per-user Startup folder

shell:SyncCenterFolder   Control Panel\All Control
Panel Items\Sync Center

shell:SyncResultsFolder   Control Panel\All Control
Panel Items\Sync Center\Sync Results

shell:SyncSetupFolder   Control Panel\All Control
Panel Items\Sync Center\Sync Setup

shell:System   C:\Windows\System32

shell:SystemCertificates
C:\Users\<username>\AppData\Roaming\Microsoft\Sy
stemCertificates

shell:SystemX86   C:\Windows\SysWOW64 -

Windows x64 only

shell:Templates
C:\Users\<username>\AppData\Roaming\Microsoft\Windows\Templates

shell:User Pinned   Pinned items for Taskbar and Start screen,
C:\Users\<username>\AppData\Roaming\Microsoft\Internet Explorer\Quick Launch\User Pinned

shell:UserProfiles
C:\Users, the users folder where the user profiles are stored

shell:UserProgramFiles   Not implemented yet. Reserved for future.

shell:UserProgramFilesCommon   same as above

shell:UsersFilesFolder   The current user profile

shell:UsersLibrariesFolder   Libraries

shell:VideosLibrary   Videos Library

shell:Windows   C:\Windows

shell:DpapiKeys
C:\Users\<username>\AppData\Roaming\Microsoft\Protect

shell:Favorites   Favorites

shell:Fonts   C:\Windows\Fonts

shell:Games   The Games Explorer item

shell:GameTasks
C:\Users\<username>\AppData\Local\Microsoft\Windows\GameExplorer

shell:History
C:\Users\<username>\AppData\Local\Microsoft\Windows\History, IE's browsing history

shell:HomeGroupCurrentUserFolder   The Home Group folder for the current user

shell:HomeGroupFolder   The Home Group root folder

shell:ImplicitAppShortcuts
C:\Users\<username>\AppData\Roaming\Microsoft\Internet Explorer\Quick Launch\User Pinned\ImplicitAppShortcuts

shell:InternetFolder   This shell command will start Internet Explorer

shell:Libraries   Libraries

shell:Links   The "Favorites" folder from the Explorer navigation pane.

shell:Local AppData
C:\Users\<username>\AppData\Local

shell:LocalAppDataLow
C:\Users\<username>\AppData\LocalLow

shell:LocalizedResourcesDir   This shell folder is broken in Windows 8

shell:MAPIFolder   Represents the Microsoft Outlook folder

shell:MusicLibrary   Music Library

shell:My Music   The "My Music" folder (not the Library)

shell:My Pictures   The "My Pictures" folder (not the Library)

shell:My Video   The "My Videos" folder (not the Library)

shell:MyComputerFolder   Computer/Drives view

shell:NetHood
C:\Users\<username>\AppData\Roaming\Microsoft\Windows\Network Shortcuts
shell:NetworkPlacesFolder   The Network Places folder which shows computers and devices on your network
shell:OEM Links   This shell command does nothing on my Windows 8 Retail edition. Maybe it works with OEM Windows 8 editions.
shell:Original Images   Not functional on Windows
shell:Personal   The "My Documents" folder (not the Library)
shell:PhotoAlbums   Saved slideshows, seems to have not been implemented yet
shell:PicturesLibrary   Pictures Library
shell:Playlists   Stores WMP Playlists.
shell:PrintersFolder   The classic "Printers" folder (not 'Devices and Printers')
shell:PrintHood
C:\Users\<username>\AppData\Roaming\Microsoft\Windows\Printer Shortcuts
shell:Profile   The User profile folder
shell:ProgramFiles   Program Files

shell:Programs
C:\Users\<username>\AppData\Roaming\Microsoft\Windows\Start Menu\Programs (Per-user Start Menu Programs folder)
shell:Public   C:\Users\Public
shell:PublicAccountPictures

C:\Users\Public\AccountPictures

shell:PublicGameTasks

C:\ProgramData\Microsoft\Windows\GameExplorer

shell:PublicLibraries   C:\Users\Public\Libraries

shell:Quick Launch

C:\Users\<username>\AppData\Roaming\Microsoft\Internet Explorer\Quick Launch

shell:Recent   The "Recent Items" folder (Recent Documents)

shell:RecordedTVLibrary   The "Recorded TV" Library

shell:RecycleBinFolder   Recycle Bin

shell:ResourceDir   C:\Windows\Resources where visual styles are stored

shell:Ringtones

C:\Users\<username>\AppData\Local\Microsoft\Windows\Ringtones

shell:Roamed Tile Images   Is not implemented yet. Reserved for future.

shell:Roaming Tiles

C:\Users\<username>\AppData\Local\Microsoft\Windows\RoamingTiles

shell:SavedGames   Saved Games

shell:Screenshots   The folder for Win+Print Screen screenshots

shell:Searches   Saved Searches

shell:SearchHomeFolder   Windows Search UI

shell:SendTo   The folder with items that you can see in the "Send to" menu

shell:Start Menu
C:\Users\<username>\AppData\Roaming\Microsoft\Windows\Start Menu (Per-user Start Menu folder)
shell:Startup   Per-user Startup folder
shell:SyncCenterFolder   Control Panel\All Control Panel Items\Sync Center
shell:SyncResultsFolder   Control Panel\All Control Panel Items\Sync Center\Sync Results
shell:SyncSetupFolder   Control Panel\All Control Panel Items\Sync Center\Sync Setup
shell:System   C:\Windows\System32
shell:SystemCertificates
C:\Users\<username>\AppData\Roaming\Microsoft\SystemCertificates
shell:SystemX86   C:\Windows\SysWOW64 - Windows x64 only
shell:Templates
C:\Users\<username>\AppData\Roaming\Microsoft\Windows\Templates
shell:User Pinned   Pinned items for Taskbar and Start screen,
C:\Users\<username>\AppData\Roaming\Microsoft\Internet Explorer\Quick Launch\User Pinned
shell:UserProfiles   C:\Users, the users folder where the user profiles are   10. stored
shell:UserProgramFiles   Not implemented yet. Reserved for future.
shell:UserProgramFilesCommon   same as above
shell:UsersFilesFolder   The current user profile

29

shell:UsersLibrariesFolder   Libraries
shell:VideosLibrary   Videos Library
shell:Windows   C:\Windows

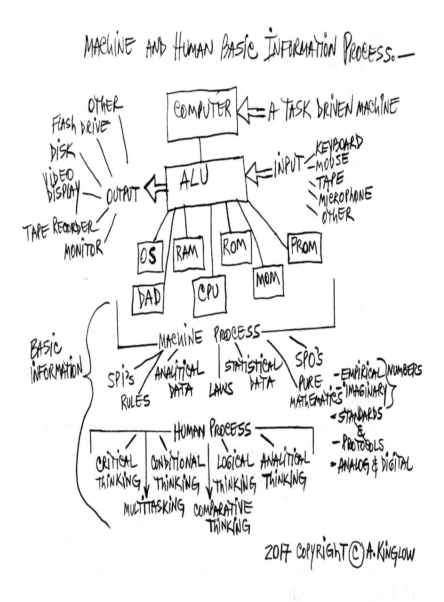

Windows Types and Versions. __

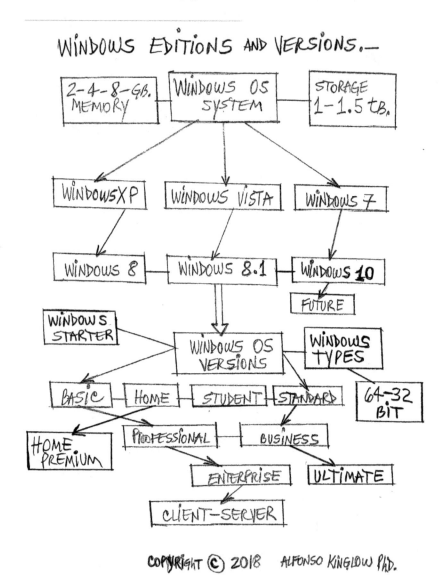

WINDOWS EDITIONS AND VERSIONS.—

3 CHAPTER THREE
WHERE IS THE COMPUTER SYSTEM INFORMATION

The Computer System Information is found in the Control Panel and is part of the System Tools. It can also be found by typing in Cortana **" System Information"** and the Desktop Application will be displayed. It can then be copied unto the Desktop.

WINDOWS SYSTEM FREE UTILITIES.___

TO KEEP YOUR COMPUTER CPU AND SYSTEM CLEAN, AND ENHANCE PERFORMANCE AND ELIMINATE MALWARE, ADAWARE AND SPYWARE.

Download the following FREE Utilities from the Internet, and Install them on your Computer. Then RUN them at least Once a Week or every two weeks:

Advanced System Care 12

Glary Utility 5.117

Clean Master 6.0

Acebyte Utility 3.2

For Virus Protection, Download the Anti Virus FREE Appllication Utility, .AVG from the Internet, and install it onto your Computer to get Virus Protection.

ALL WINDOWS   BUILT IN TOOLS.

Windows User Tools

1. Command prompt

2. Control Panel

3. Resource Monitor

4. Run Command

5. Slide to Shutdown

6. System Information

7. Task Manager

8. Safe Mode Shift + F8

9. Special Menu Windows Key + "X" Key

10. Shell

Windows Diagnostic Tools:

2. MSConfig from RUN

3. 3D Builder

4. Narrator

5. Performance monitor

6. Resource Monitor

7. RUN Command

8. System Configuration

9. Task Manager

Windows System Tools:

On Screen Keyboard

Phone companion

Phone

System Information

Uninstall

Windows Memory Diagnostic Tools

Win Patrol Explorer

Win Patrol Help

CMD Command Line

Windows Administrative Tools

1. Computer Management

2. Defragment drives

3. Disk Cleanup

4. Event Viewer

5. ISCSI Initiator

6. Local Security Policy

7. ODBC Data Sources

8. Performance Monitor

9. Print Management

10.   Recovery Drive

11.   Resource Monitor

12.   Services

13.   System Configuration

14.   System Information

15.   Task Scheduler

16.   Windows defender Firewall

17.   Windows Memory Diagnostic

18.   To get more **Performance** from Windows, type **sysdm.cpl** using the RUN command, a window will be displayed; then goto Settings in the Performance Tab.

WINDOWS USER TOOLS.

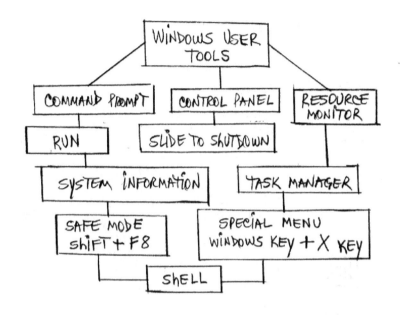

COMPUTER VIRUSSES.—

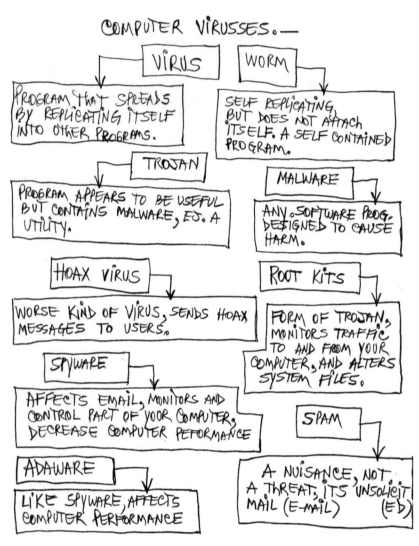

VIRUS
PROGRAM THAT SPREADS BY REPLICATING ITSELF INTO OTHER PROGRAMS.

WORM
SELF REPLICATING, BUT DOES NOT ATTACH ITSELF. A SELF CONTAINED PROGRAM.

TROJAN
PROGRAM APPEARS TO BE USEFUL BUT CONTAINS MALWARE, E.G. A UTILITY.

MALWARE
ANY SOFTWARE PROG. DESIGNED TO CAUSE HARM.

HOAX VIRUS
WORSE KIND OF VIRUS, SENDS HOAX MESSAGES TO USERS.

ROOT KITS
FORM OF TROJAN, MONITORS TRAFFIC TO AND FROM YOUR COMPUTER, AND ALTERS SYSTEM FILES.

SPYWARE
AFFECTS EMAIL, MONITORS AND CONTROL PART OF YOUR COMPUTER, DECREASE COMPUTER PEFORMANCE

SPAM
A NUISANCE, NOT A THREAT, ITS UNSOLICIT MAIL (E-MAIL)   (ED)

ADAWARE
LIKE SPYWARE, AFFECTS COMPUTER PERFORMANCE

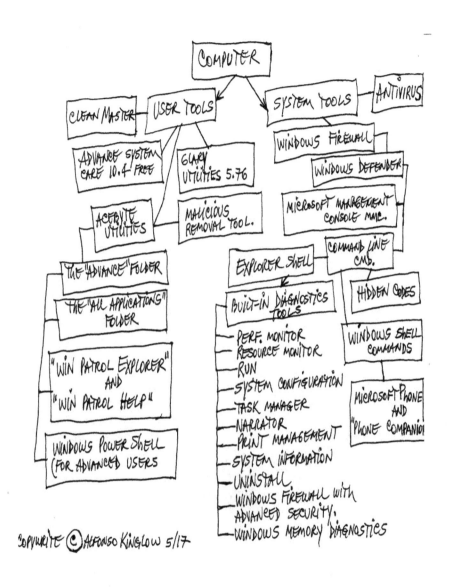

COMPUTER

CLEAN MASTER — USER TOOLS

SYSTEM TOOLS — ANTIVIRUS

ADVANCE SYSTEM CARE 10.4 FREE

GLARY UTILITIES 5.76

WINDOWS FIREWALL

WINDOWS DEFENDER

ACEBYTE UTILITIES

MALICIOUS REMOVAL TOOL.

MICROSOFT MANAGEMENT CONSOLE MMC.

THE "ADVANCE" FOLDER

EXPLORER SHELL

COMMAND LINE CMD.

THE "ALL APPLICATIONS" FOLDER

BUILT-IN DIAGNOSTICS TOOLS

HIDDEN CODES

"WIN PATROL EXPLORER" AND "WIN PATROL HELP"

- PERF. MONITOR
- RESOURCE MONITOR
- RUN
- SYSTEM CONFIGURATION
- TASK MANAGER
- NARRATOR
- PRINT MANAGEMENT
- SYSTEM INFORMATION
- UNINSTALL
- WINDOWS FIREWALL WITH ADVANCED SECURITY.
- WINDOWS MEMORY DIAGNOSTICS

WINDOWS SHELL COMMANDS

WINDOWS POWER SHELL (FOR ADVANCED USERS

MICROSOFT PHONE AND "PHONE COMPANION

COMPUTER VIRUSES PART TWO.

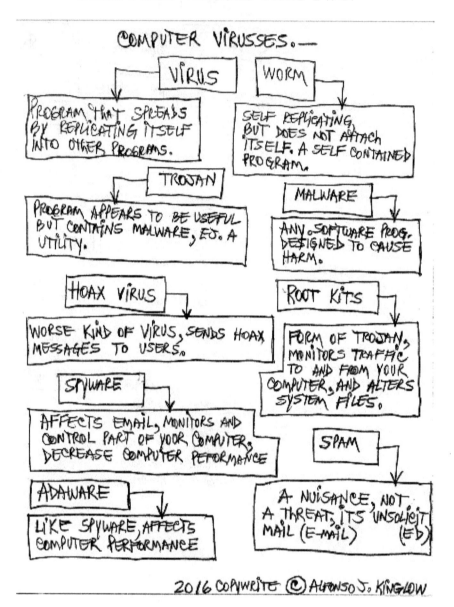

COMPUTER VIRUSSES.—

VIRUS
PROGRAM THAT SPREADS BY REPLICATING ITSELF INTO OTHER PROGRAMS.

WORM
SELF REPLICATING, BUT DOES NOT ATTACH ITSELF. A SELF CONTAINED PROGRAM.

TROJAN
PROGRAM APPEARS TO BE USEFUL BUT CONTAINS MALWARE, EJ. A UTILITY.

MALWARE
ANY SOFTWARE PROG. DESIGNED TO CAUSE HARM.

HOAX VIRUS
WORSE KIND OF VIRUS, SENDS HOAX MESSAGES TO USERS.

ROOT KITS
FORM OF TROJAN, MONITORS TRAFFIC TO AND FROM YOUR COMPUTER, AND ALTERS SYSTEM FILES.

SPYWARE
AFFECTS EMAIL, MONITORS AND CONTROL PART OF YOUR COMPUTER, DECREASE COMPUTER PERFORMANCE

SPAM

ADAWARE
LIKE SPYWARE, AFFECTS COMPUTER PERFORMANCE

A NUISANCE, NOT A THREAT, ITS UNSOLICIT MAIL (E-MAIL)   (ED)

2016 COPYWRITE © ALFONSO J. KINGLOW

42

TYPES OF COMPUTER BATTERIES FOR COMPUTER SYSTEMS.____

POLYMER   FLASHLITE/ OTHER DEVICES

LITHIUM-ION   Laptops/ Desktops/ Most Devices

CERAMIC Laptops/ Desktops /other devices

MAGNESIUM Laptops/Desktops /Special Devices

BATTERY FOR COMPUTERS.___

Lithium-ion batteries are popular because they have a number of important **advantages** over competing technologies:

They're generally much lighter than other types of rechargeable batteries of the same size. The electrodes of a lithium-ion battery are made of lightweight **lithium** and **carbon**. Lithium is also a highly reactive element, meaning that a lot of energy can be stored in its atomic bonds. This translates into a very high **energy density** for lithium-ion batteries. Here is a way to get a perspective on the energy density. A typical lithium-ion battery can store 150 watt-hours of electricity in 1 kilogram of battery. A **NiMH (nickel-metal hydride) battery** pack can store perhaps 100 watt-hours per kilogram, although 60 to 70 watt-hours might be more typical. A **lead-acid battery** can store only 25 watt-hours per kilogram. Using lead-acid technology, it takes 6 kilograms to store the same amount of energy that a 1 kilogram lithium-ion battery can handle. That's a huge difference.

They hold their charge. A lithium-ion battery pack loses only about 5 percent of its charge per month, compared to a 20 percent loss per month for NiMH batteries.

They have no **memory effect**, which means that you

do not have to completely discharge them before recharging, as with some other <u>battery chemistries</u>.

Lithium-ion batteries can handle hundreds of charge/discharge cycles.

That is not to say that lithium-ion batteries are flawless. They have a few disadvantages as well:

DISADVANTAGES:

They start degrading as soon as they leave the factory. They will **only last two or three years** from the date of manufacture whether you use them or not.

They are extremely sensitive to high temperatures. Heat causes lithium-ion battery packs to degrade much faster than they normally would.

If you completely discharge a lithium-ion battery, it is ruined.

A lithium-ion battery pack must have an on-board computer to manage the battery. This makes them even more expensive than they already are.

There is a small chance that, if a lithium-ion battery pack fails, it will burst into flame.

Many of these characteristics can be understood by looking at the chemistry inside a lithium-ion cell

The positive electrode is made of Lithium cobalt oxide, or **$LiCoO_2$.** The negative electrode is made of carbon. When the battery charges, ions of lithium move through the electrolyte from the positive electrode to the negative electrode and attach to the carbon. During discharge, the lithium ions move back to the **LiCoO2** from the carbon.

The movement of these lithium ions happens at a fairly high voltage, so each cell produces 3.7 volts. This is much higher than the 1.5 volts typical of a normal AA alkaline cell that you buy at the supermarket and helps make lithium-ion batteries more compact in small devices like cell phones.

Rugged Ceramic Batteries Deliver 3X Leap in Capacity, Operate At 120°C and Beyond

Lee H. Goldberg

A recently-announced solid-state battery technology may enable manufacturers to deliver up to three times more energy than equivalent-sized lithium-ion (Li-ion) cell, while eliminating many of the durability and safety issues associated with conventional lithium-based energy sources. The technology, developed by <u>Johnson Battery Technologies (JBT)</u>, Atlanta, GA, employs ceramic electrolytes instead of volatile liquid or gel electrolytes. "Our team has spent countless hours in the lab perfecting a battery technology that will truly change the game for safe energy storage across a variety of applications," states Dr. Lonnie Johnson, a former NASA scientist and JBT's CEO and Founder.

After producing several generations of prototype cells and delivering evaluation units to one of its affiliates, Johnson says that his company is ready to partner with industry and government customers to bring the batteries to the marketplace. Although JBT's initial target markets will be limited to micro-batteries and specialized high-temperature industrial applications, their long-term plans include developing batteries for portableelectronics, electric vehicles a__Prototype JBT ceramic batteries undergoing high-temperature testing.nd large-scale energy storage.

A JBT cell consists of a solid ceramic cathode material, a high-conductivity glass electrolyte and a lithium metal anode, which produces a working voltage of 4V. The unique chemistry has already demonstrated energy densities of 1100-1200 Watt-Hours per Liter (WH/l). This is expected to increase to around 2000 as the technology matures. In contrast, most commercially-available (Li-ion) batteries deliver only 500-600 WH/l.

The solid-state battery's chemistry reverses very cleanly, enabling test units to successfully undergo many thousands of charge/discharge cycles with minimal degradation in capacity. In addition, JBT cells can withstand higher and lower voltages than most conventional batteries and are designed for significantly lower self-discharge than conventional (Li-ion) batteries.

Using a solid electrolyte eliminates the passive corrosion problems, which make conventional (li-ion) chemistry prone to catching fire or exploding. It is also well suited for harsh environments and has already enabled prototypes to demonstrate reliable operation beyond 120°C (250°F). This, and the high-temperature hermetic packaging developed for the cells allows them to survive autoclave, pasteurization and other industrial processes. JBT's solid-state lithium-metal chemistry has been tested in very severe environments, undergoing drilling, boiling water and other stress testing. Under no circumstance did the battery catch fire or explode, unlike current battery technologies on the market.

With the technology still in its early stages, it will be a while before you will see ceramic batteries powering cell phones, power tools or electric vehicles. However, there are several areas where their unique advantages already give them a big advantage over existing solutions. Solid state batteries' durability, reliability and wide operating temperature range makes them an ideal fit for many industrial applications, especially in field equipment used by oil and gas companies. For example, JBT has already designed and delivered prototypes of a battery to power a pressure temperature gauge. The company has also been approached about developing a battery to be used in a sensor for the monitoring of oilfield cement curing.

JBT is also targeting the micro-battery market where they feel they have several significant advantages over the thin-film printed battery technologies used to manufacture today's products. The current crop of thin film cells offered by companies such as Cymbet are fabricated using relatively costly sputtering techniques to deposit a thin film cathode and electrolyte onto a ceramic substrate. The resulting products, used in remote sensors, IoT devices and small energy harvesting systems offer capacities in the 5-100 μA-hour range with maximum operating temperatures of -40 to 70°C. In contrast, JBT has demonstrated high-temperature batteries with an equivalent footprint that offer capacities of up to 1000+ μA-hours.

Watch a video on Revolutionary designs for energy alternatives: Lonnie Johnson at TEDxAtlanta.

CEO Johnson says that as the battery technology

matures, JBT plans to expand their capacity to 10's hundreds, and thousands of Watt-Hours for use in portable equipment, vehicles, and energy storage systems. "These robust, high-capacity cells will be a perfect complement to the **advanced thermo-electric generating system** we're developing at our sister company, Johnson R&D" he says. "Together, they provide a cost-effective renewable power source that's available on a 24/7 basis. And that means a greener, more hopeful future for all of us".

For more information, contact the company at info@johnsonbatterytech.com or visit JBT's web site at http://johnsonbatterytech.com/.

4 CHAPTER FOUR
START UP AND SHUTDOWN WINDOWS

There is a <u>correct</u> way to shutdown Windows after Startup. When Windows startup it goes thru a process of checking all the components in the ALU, specially the Memory, CPU and Storage that is available and installed in the computer hardware.

There is a hidden SHUTDOWN application in Windows that will correctly Shutdown Windows like a Curtain blinds that you Pull Down to close it and Pull up to open the blinds. It is called: **SLIDE TO SHUTDOWN.EXE**

This hidden application is found in the C:> Drive on the computer,
in the folder <u>C:>/Windows/System32/shutdown.exe</u>

Slide to Shutdown.exe Utility is Located in:
<u>C:/</u> **windows/system32 on the Hard Drive.** Copy it
to the Desktop.

The other way is to call the TASK MANAGER by
holding down at the same time the; Control+ Alt+
Del Keys on the Keyboard., and then clicking on the
Power Button to the bottom right of the Task
Manager window on the desktop.

The Power button is the round circle with the dot in
the center.

The other conventional way of shutting down is to
press the Shutdown tab on the Start Button in the

lower left side of the computer desktop.

Never Shutdown the Computer by closing the Lid. Windows will not be able to close down all of its Modules that are running and the OS could be damage or delayed the next time you try to Start Windows.

The Power Options should be configured in the Control Panel to prevent this. The selection should be **NEVER, NEVER** for both when on **Battery** and when **Plugged-in.**

Never, Never should be selected for everything; all the **Power Options.** NEVER put the computer to **SLEEP.**

POWER OPTION SETTINGS. __

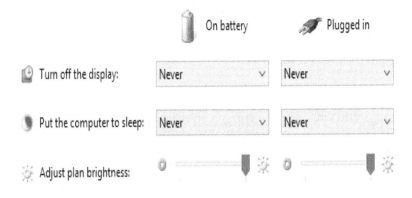

Change settings for the plan: Balanced

Choose the sleep and display settings that you want your computer to use.

	On battery	Plugged in
🕐 Turn off the display:	Never ∨	Never ∨
🌙 Put the computer to sleep:	Never ∨	Never ∨
☼ Adjust plan brightness:	○ ━━━━ 🔅	○ ━━━━ 🔅

The Power Option Setup is done in the Control Panel.

Auto Play will need to be setup and configured in the Control Panel also, so that the CD/DVD Player can work correctly with Windows Software and Operating System.

MORE PERFORMANCE FROM WINDOWS. __

To get more Performance from Windows, from the RUN

Command; type the command: **sysdm.cpl**

Select the Advanced Tab and then the system properties window will be displayed showing Performance, User Profile and Startup and Recovery.

Select Performance Settings, to Display all of the Settings for Performance and Appearance, and choose what you want Windows to do.

Performance Options

Visual Effects   Advanced   Data Execution Prevention

Select the settings you want to use for the appearance and performance of Windows on this computer.

○ Let Windows choose what's best for my computer

○ Adjust for best appearance

○ Adjust for best performance

◉ Custom:

- ☑ Animate controls and elements inside windows
- ☐ Animate windows when minimizing and maximizing
- ☐ Animations in the taskbar
- ☑ Enable Peek
- ☑ Fade or slide menus into view
- ☑ Fade or slide ToolTips into view
- ☑ Fade out menu items after clicking
- ☑ Save taskbar thumbnail previews
- ☐ Show shadows under mouse pointer
- ☐ Show shadows under windows
- ☑ Show thumbnails instead of icons
- ☐ Show translucent selection rectangle
- ☐ Show window contents while dragging
- ☑ Slide open combo boxes
- ☑ Smooth edges of screen fonts
- ☑ Smooth-scroll list boxes
- ☐ Use drop shadows for icon labels on the desktop

Windows Performance Tool. PERFMON.

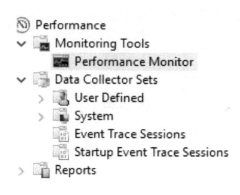
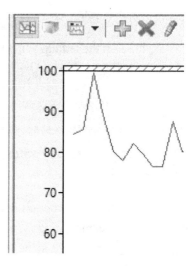

5 CHAPTER FIVE
ALL WINDOWS BUILT IN TOOLS

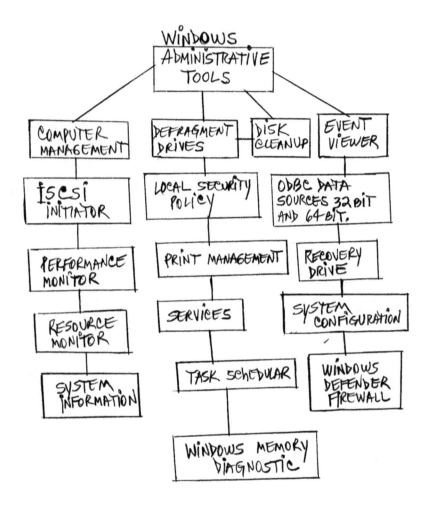

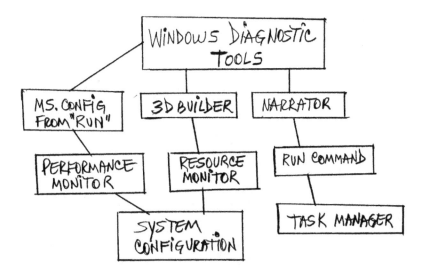

WINDOWS SYSTEM TOOLS BUILT-IN.__

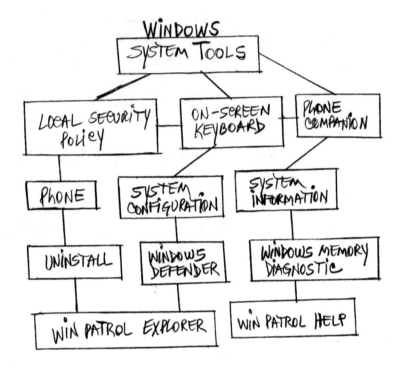

WINDOWS USER TOOLS BUILT-IN. _

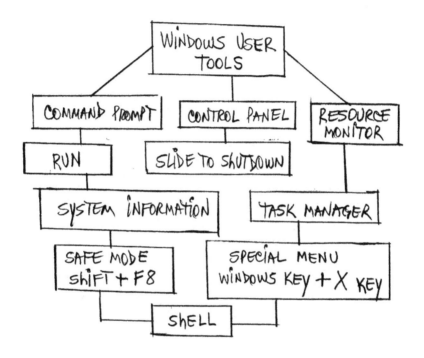

WINDOWS TOOLS BUILT- IN. __

 Command Prompt
Shortcut
1.50 KB

 Control Panel
Shortcut
405 bytes

 Resource Monitor
Shortcut
1.08 KB

 Run
Shortcut
409 bytes

 SlideToShutDown
SlideToShutDown
Microsoft Corporation

 System Information
Shortcut
1.08 KB

 Task Manager
Shortcut
1.66 KB

 Windows Shortcuts and Special Menu
Microsoft Word 97-2003 D...

ADMINISTRATIVE TOOLS BUILT- IN. __

GPEDIT.MSC

SECPOL.MSC

Administrative Tools
Shortcut
918 bytes

Local Security Policy
Shortcut
1.09 KB

SecEdit
Windows Security Configur...
Microsoft Corporation

SlideToShutDown
SlideToShutDown
Microsoft Corporation

WINDOWS TOOLS BUILT-IN. __

 dxdiag
Microsoft DirectX Diagnost...
Microsoft Corporation

 On-Screen Keyboard
Shortcut
2.10 KB

 Phone Companion
Shortcut
1.64 KB

 Phone
Shortcut
1.47 KB

 System Information
Shortcut
1.97 KB

 Uninstall
Shortcut
1.81 KB

 **Windows Memory
Diagnostic**
Shortcut

 WinPatrol Explorer
Shortcut
1.93 KB

 WinPatrol Help
Shortcut
1.90 KB

6 CHAPTER SIX

WINDOWS EDITIONS AND VERSIONS.

WINDOWS EDITIONS AND VERSIONS.—

2-4-8-GB. MEMORY	WINDOWS OS SYSTEM	STORAGE 1-1.5 tB.

WINDOWS XP — WINDOWS VISTA — WINDOWS 7

WINDOWS 8 — WINDOWS 8.1 — WINDOWS 10

FUTURE

WINDOWS STARTER

WINDOWS OS VERSIONS

WINDOWS TYPES

BASIC — HOME — STUDENT — STANDARD

64-32 BIT

HOME PREMIUM

PROFESSIONAL — BUSINESS

ENTERPRISE

ULTIMATE

CLIENT-SERVER

GETTING THE HIDDEN BATTERY REPORT IN WINDOWS
10, 7 and 8.____

The active **Status** of the Battery on the User Computer can be obtained using the **CMD Command Line Utility** built into Windows., and running the Utility as **Administrator.**

Type CMD in the Startup Window in Windows, then make a <u>shortcut</u> of the CMD desktop App; **right click** on it and select" Run as Administrator" then type: **powercfg /batteryreport** and press <Enter>

The file on the Hard Drive in C:\windows\system 32\batteryreport.html <u>will be created.</u>

Copy the file to the Desktop to Print or View it.

Go to C:\windows\system 32 folder and look for the file; *battery_report* that was just created on the C Drive to Print it or View it.

BASIC COMPUTER SPECS FOR A NEW COMPUTER.

Desktop or Laptop.

<u>Windows 10 Professional</u> – 64 Bit <u>Operating System</u> , <u>Recommended</u>

 <u>Processor</u>: **INTEL Dual Core** – i-5, i-7, or i-9

(Do Not Buy Computers with AMD Processors.)

<u>Installed RAM Memory</u>: **8GB DDR3** minimum. (Do not buy Computers with 3 GB. of Memory; or 6GB of Memory. (Memory Standard is 1, 2, 4, 8, 16, 32, 64, 128 GB. Etc.. (3 GB and 6 GB does not conform to the Memory Standard.)

<u>Storage Hard Drive</u> C:> must be at least 1 TB. (One Terabyte) or more...

<u>Network Card:</u> Must be **802.11 AC** (the New

Standard) for Wi-Fi. And for Wired Network: Gigabit Ethernet Card. Do not buy Computers with **802.11**

a/b/n Card for Wi Fi Networks, as its outdated and very slow.

Graphic Card: **NVIDIA** or **ATI HD** Graphics or better

Video Display Screen: **15.4** Inches or **17** inch wide. Twenty Inch or higher Monitor, for use with Desktop Towers.

Hardware Brands: **LENOVO**, **HP**, SAMSUNG, SONY, TOSHIBA,DELL

Computers are Sold at: **Walmart, Best Buy, Staples, Office Max, Costco or On Line via the Internet.**

COMPUTER VIRUSES UPDATED. __

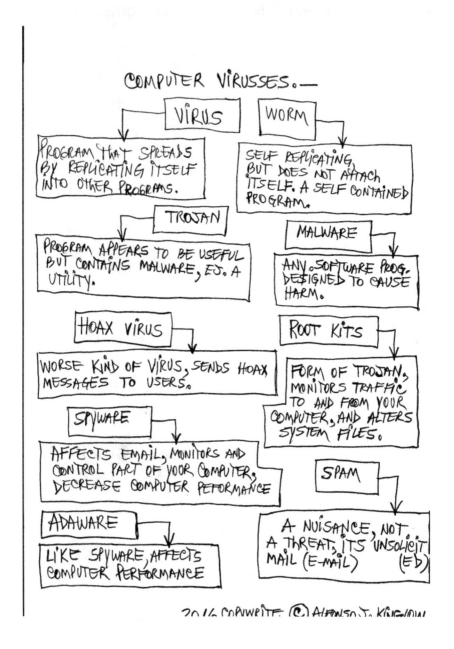

COMPUTER VIRUSSES.—

VIRUS

PROGRAM THAT SPREADS BY REPLICATING ITSELF INTO OTHER PROGRAMS.

WORM

SELF REPLICATING, BUT DOES NOT ATTACH ITSELF. A SELF CONTAINED PROGRAM.

TROJAN

PROGRAM APPEARS TO BE USEFUL BUT CONTAINS MALWARE, EJ. A UTILITY.

MALWARE

ANY SOFTWARE PROG. DESIGNED TO CAUSE HARM.

HOAX VIRUS

WORSE KIND OF VIRUS, SENDS HOAX MESSAGES TO USERS.

ROOT KITS

FORM OF TROJAN, MONITORS TRAFFIC TO AND FROM YOUR COMPUTER, AND ALTERS SYSTEM FILES.

SPYWARE

AFFECTS EMAIL, MONITORS AND CONTROL PART OF YOOR COMPUTER, DECREASE COMPUTER PETFORMANCE

SPAM

ADAWARE

LIKE SPYWARE, AFFECTS COMPUTER PERFORMANCE

A NUISANCE, NOT A THREAT, ITS UNSOLICIT MAIL (E-MAIL)   (ED)

2016 COPYWRITE (C) ALFONSO J. KINGLOW

Create the Special Advance Folder.__

The Special Advanced folder is the most important Folder that will ever be created. This folder contains over 220 files that are Tabulated and Organized to Help the User Resolve any and all problems with Windows.

When the Folder is created it will be different from any Windows Folder. It will be Green or Blue, with symbols.

Follow the instructions to Create this Folder, which is Recommended for all Users.

CREATE A NEW FOLDER, CALL IT: **ADVANCED.**

Put a Period. After the **D.**

ENTER THE CODE AFTER YOU OPEN BRACKET, CLOSE BRACKET AT THE END.

OPEN BRACKET{

CLOSE BRACKET}

Advanced.{ED7BA470-8E54-465E-825C-99712043E01C}   <ENTER>

CHAPTER SEVEN
MMC MICROSOFT MANAGEMENT CONSOLE.

The Microsoft Management Console (MMC) Windows Tool for Users and Administrators. A Basic Admin tool.

Step-by-Step Guide to the Microsoft Management Console for Users Beginners.

The Microsoft Management Console **(MMC)** lets system administrators and Users create much more flexible user interfaces and customize administration tools. This step-by-step guide explores some of these new features.

Introduction

MMC unifies and simplifies day-to-day system management tasks. It hosts tools and displays them as consoles. These tools, consisting of one or more applications, are built with modules called **Snap-ins.** The snap-ins also can include additional extension snap-ins. MMC is a core part of Microsoft's management strategy and is included in Microsoft Windows® operating systems. In addition,

Microsoft development groups will use MMC for future management applications.

Microsoft Management Console enables system users to create special tools to delegate specific administrative tasks to users or groups. Microsoft provides standard tools with the operating system that perform everyday administrative tasks that users need to accomplish. These are part of the **All Users** profile of the computer and located in the **Administrative Tools** group on the **Startup** menu. Saved as MMC console (.msc) files, these custom tools can be sent by e-mail, shared in a network folder, or posted on the Web. They can also be assigned to users, groups, or computers with system policy settings. A tool can be scaled up and down, integrated seamlessly into the operating system, repackaged, and customized.

Using MMC, system administrators can create unique consoles for workers who report to them or for workgroup managers. They can assign a tool with a system policy, deliver the file by e-mail, or post the file to a shared location on the network. When a workgroup manager opens the .msc file, access will be restricted to those tools provided by the system administrator.

Building your own tools with the standard user interface in MMC is a straightforward process. Start with an existing console and modify or add components to fulfill your needs. Or create an entirely new console. The following example shows how to create a new console and arrange its administrative components into separate windows.

Prerequisites and Requirements

There are no prerequisites: <u>you don't need to complete any other step-by-step guide</u> before starting this guide. You need one computer running either Windows Professional or Windows Server. For the most current information about hardware requirements and compatibility for servers, clients, and peripherals, see the Check Hardware and Software Compatibility page on the Windows website.

Creating Consoles

The most common way for administrators to use MMC is to simply start a predefined console file from the Start menu. However, to get an idea of the flexibility of MMC, it is useful to create a console file from scratch. It is also useful to create a console file from scratch when using the new task delegation features in this version of MMC.

Creating a New Console File

On the Start Menu, click **Run**, type **MMC**, and then click **OK**. Microsoft Management Console opens with an empty console (or administrative tool) as shown in Figure 1 below. The empty console has no management functionality until you add some snap-ins. The MMC menu commands on the menu bar at the top of the Microsoft Management Console window apply to the entire console.

Figure 1: Beginning Console Window

Click Console (under Console1). On the Console Menu, click **Add/Remove Snap-in**. The Add/Remove Snap-in dialog box opens. This lets you enable extensions and configure which snap-ins are in the console file. You can specify where the snap-ins should be inserted in the **Snap-in's "added to** drop-down box." Accept the default, **Console Root**, for this exercise.

Click **Add**. This displays the Add Standalone Snap-in dialog box that lists the snap-ins that are installed on your computer.

From the list of snap-ins, double-click **Computer Management** to open the **Computer Management** wizard.

Click **Local computer** and select the check box for **"Allow the selected computer to be changed when launching from the command line."**

Click **Finish**. This returns you to the **Add/Remove Snap-ins** dialog box. Click **Close**.

Click the **Extensions** tab as shown in Figure 2 below. By selecting the check box **Add all extensions**, all locally-installed extensions on the computer are used. If this check box is not selected, then any extension snap-in that is selected is explicitly loaded when the console file is opened on a different computer.

Figure 2: Select All Extensions

Click **OK** to close the Add/Remove Snap-in dialog box. The Console Root window now has a snap-in, **Computer Management**, rooted at the Console Root folder.

Customizing the Display of Snap-ins in the Console:

New Windows

After you add the snap-ins, you can add windows to provide different administrative views in the console.

To add windows

In the left pane of the tree view in Figure 3 below, click the **+** next to **Computer Management.** Click **System Tools**.

■

Figure 3: Console1: System Tools

Right-click the **Event Viewer** folder that opens, and then click **New window** from here. As shown in Figure 4 below, this opens a new Event Viewer window rooted at the Event Viewer extension to computer management.

Figure 4: Event Viewer

Click **Window** and click **Console Root**.

In the Console Root window, click **Services and Applications**, right-click **Services** in the left pane, and then click **New Window**. As shown in Figure 5 below, this opens a new Services window rooted at the Event Viewer extension to Computer Management. In the new window, click the

Show/Hide Console Tree toolbar button to hide the console tree, as shown in the red circle in Figure 5 below.

▫

Figure 5: Show/Hide Button

Close the original window with Console Root showing in it.

On the Window menu, select **Tile Horizontally**. The console file should appear and include the information shown in Figure 4 and Figure 5 above.

You can now save your new MMC console. Click the **Save as** icon on the Console window, and give your console a name. Your console is now saved as a .msc file, and you can provide it to anyone who needs to configure a computer with these tools.

Note: Each of the two smaller windows has a toolbar with buttons and drop-down menus. The toolbar buttons and drop-down menus on these each of these two windows apply only to the contents of the window. You can see that a window's toolbar buttons and menus change depending on the snap-in selected in the left pane of the window. If you select the View menu, you can see a list of available toolbars.

Tip: The windows fit better if your monitor display

is set to a higher resolution and small font.

Creating Console Taskpads

If you are creating a console file for another user, it's useful to provide a very simplified view with only a few tasks available. Console taskpads help you to do this.

To create a console taskpad

From the Window menu, select **New Window.** Close the other two windows (you will save a new console file at the end of this procedure). Maximize the remaining window.

In the left pane, click the **+** next to the **Computer Management** folder, then click the **+** next to the **System Tools** folder. Click **System**, click the **Event Viewer** folder, right-click **System**, and select **New Taskpad** View.

Go through the wizard accepting all the default settings. Verify the checkbox on the last page is checked so that the Task Creation wizard can start automatically.

Choose the defaults in the Task Creation wizard until you come to the page shown below in Figure 6, then choose a list view task and select **Properties:**

Figure 6: New Task Wizard

Click **Next** and accept the defaults for the rest of the screens. By selecting an Event and clicking **Properties**, you can see the property page for that Event.

After you click **Finish** on the last screen, your console should look like Figure 7 below:

Figure 7: New Console Showing System Event Log

Click the **Show/Hide console tree** toolbar button.

From the view menu, click **Customize** and click each of the options except the Description bar to hide each type of toolbar.

The next section discusses how to lock the console file down so that the user sees only a limited view. For right now your console file should look like Figure 8 below.

Figure 8: Customized View

Setting Console File Options

If you are creating a console file for another user, it is useful to prevent that user from further customizing the console file. The Options dialog box allows you to do this.

To set console file options

From the **Console** menu, select **Options**.

Change the Console Mode by selecting **User Modelimited access, single window** from the drop-down dialog box. This will prevent a user from adding new snap-ins to the console file or rearranging the windows.

You can change the name from Console1. Click **OK** to continue.

Save the console file. The changes will not take effect until the console file is opened again.

This is just one example of how the Microsoft Management Console lets you group information and functionality that previously would have required opening a Control Panel option plus two separate administrative tools. The modular architecture of MMC makes it easy for system network users and beginners to create snap-in applications that leverage the platform while easing administrative load.

8 CHAPTER EIGHT

Protecting your Computer.__

You can protect your computer by installing a free or paid version of an Antivirus program. Many Antivirus programs are available from different manufacturers, they all protect your computer when properly installed, and with the Virus Definition file updated. A first time Scan is required before the program can begin to protect your computer. Before you start the next Scan, after you have done your first Scan, make sure that you are disconnected from the Internet, and or turn off momentarily your router. Then you may Scan your computer again.

The first time you Scan your computer you need to be connected to the Internet so that your Virus Definition file can get updated.

It is advisable to Scan your computer at least once a week.

A Security software program is not an Antivirus program and does not offer any protection against the many viruses that are a threat. Some Security software programs claim to protect your

computer from viruses, only an Antivirus software program will protect your computer from viruses.

Your Computer Security. ___

Windows 7 and 8 comes with some security protection. The new Windows 10 operating system have a new complete security configuration that is presented here as part of the Revision.

They are two main Security modules in the Control Panel, one of them is called; Windows Defender and the other is Windows Firewall. Make sure that they are both turned on and are working. Your Firewall must be always on to protect your computer from threats.

Firewalls can be internal or external, and can be software and or hardware. Having an external Firewall box will greatly enhance the security protection to your computer.

The Control Panel in Windows 7 - 8 and 10.

The Control Panel is the heart of your computer. All the modules running in the Control Panel are performing a function so that your computer may run smoothly.

To access the Control Panel, go to the Start or Run button in the lower left side of your Desktop, and select Settings, if the Control Panel is not visible in the menu, to bring up the Control Panel or if you are running Windows 8 you may also go to the Folder on the lower left side of your Desktop, and click on Computer, and the Control Panel will be displayed in the center Tabs that are visible. The Control Panel

Icon Folder is unique and very different from any other folders.

Administrative Users vs. Standard Users

In the Control Panel one of the most important controls is the User's Control Panel, where you can Create new Users for your computer and edit existing users. It is recommended that you

first create a New User, when you get your computer for the first time. This New User would most likely be you. Once the user is created, you need to give the New User Administrative Rights, so that the user may have full control of the Computer.

This user will then become the User Administrator. A Standard User will not have rights and privileges on the computer to do anything. As the Owner of your computer, you need to have full rights on your machine. Otherwise you will not be able to install or remove any software or do basic maintenance on your own machine, so this is a very first most important step, after getting your computer.

System Administrator vs. User Administrator

It is very important to know what is the System Administrator Password. If the Windows System Software gets corrupted, and needs to be re-installed; you will need to know the Administrator Password in order to get into the System to perform general maintenance and re

installation of the system software. When Windows is installed for the first time on any machine, in the installation process, a password is requested for the *Administrator,* this password is important to know and remember, if you did not install your system and some one else did it; then you might be out of luck if you do not know the Administrator Password or Admin password.

Most computers come with the Windows OS already installed, so the Admin password is not known. It is therefore important to get the original Windows Re-installation DVD, so that you may reinstall Windows if it gets corrupted or crashes.

Every new Computer should be provided with the Installation DVD included in the "sealed" Box and not in a Box with a Tape over it, which indicates that the Box was opened, and that the original DVD, Manuals and other User Documentation was taken out.

Please note this as it is obvious that the Computer was not shipped to the store in a box with a Tape around it. All Computers are shipped in "sealed" boxes, there is no Tape involved.

The User Administrator only has rights and privileges over the user's machine and does not have any System administrator rights over any of the System software.

If the user tries to change, alter, modify etc.. Any system applications; a message will be displayed alerting the "User" that he or she does not have any rights or privilege to make or do the changes they want.

Please note that the User with Administrative privileges is not the same as the User Administrator.

COMPUTER NETWORKS, NETWORKING AND

THE COMPUTER NETWORK CARDS OR ADAPTERS.

Let us define what Computer Networks are first, any computer that is connected to any other computer to share files and other applications is said to be connected to a Network. When computers need to share files and other software they are connected together in a LAN. A LAN is a Local Area Network. To facilitate this configuration, all computers have built in Network Cards.

They are two kinds of Network Cards also called NIC's, The first card or NIC is the " Ethernet Card" This is a special card that meets the International Standard for Networking called Ethernet (IEE 802.3) or Project 802, which is an IEEE Standard, accepted worldwide. The speed of this network card is 100 Mbps or 1 Gbps.,(Gigabit Ethernet) or higher.The Gigabit Ethernet card is much faster than the 100 Mbps card and is desirable.

WIRELESS CARD OR ADAPTER. __

The second Network card is the Wireless card or WiFi card (802.11b/g/n) and the new standard ac/ and /ad.

So the built in Wireless card should be (802.11 b/g/n or 802.11 b/g/n/AC or AD. This is the new Wireless Standard for the Network Card that is preferred, a new Standard is been developed and will be available in 2019; if you want to have a fast Network connection. If your Wireless card does not meet this standard, then it will be very slow and you will not be able to connect to the Internet. Your Wireless built in card must be at least (802.11 b/g/n) or higher.

Computers connect to the Internet through these cards. The connection to and from these cards is called Networking.

The settings for your Wireless and Ethernet cards are in the Control Panel, and it's called: "Networking and Sharing Center".

Networking is divided into LAN (Local Area Networks) and WAN (Wide Area Networks); The largest WAN in the world is the Internet.

Wireless adapters or cards are also installed into Printers which makes them " Wireless Printers"

Most printers are now Wireless and require no cables, most printers are supplied with a USB (Universal Serial Bus) Cable, which is another Standard used in computers and networking.

WAN Networking requires special equipment and meets different standards with different kinds of cables and interfaces.

THE NETWORKING MODEL

Networking is based on a Model accepted worldwide; it's called the OSI Networking Model or Open Systems Interconnect. Computer Network cards and Networking in general must follow this Model. All network cards are assigned a network protocol number or network ID that identifies the card on the Network. It is a special hexadecimal number (numbers and letters combined), this is also called in networking an IP

(Internet Protocol) Address. This IP identifies the computer on a Network and is part of the

Internet Protocol (TCP/IP) a Networking Standard. Without a TCP/IP address number the computer can not connect to the Internet or Network.

The speed of the computer Internet connection will depend on the built in Network cards. To find out what kind of Network cards is installed in your computer; go to the Control Panel to Network and Sharing Center and select "change adapter settings" to display the type and kind of network cards installed in the computer.   A.

Networks and the Internet. _____

Networks are used to join computers and devices together and to share resources.

The type of resources that are shared are: Information, Hardware, Software, and Data.

A Hardware resource that is shared could be a

single connected Printer, that is shared via the Network to multiple Computers. These are shared through a LAN (Local Area Network) or a WAN (Wide Area Network.)

To access the Internet services the user can connect via an ISP (Internet Service Provider) or via an OSP (Online Service Provider).

The main Internet Service is the World Wide Web (WWW.) and the Internet is the largest Network in the World.

The Internet is a worldwide collection of Networks that links individuals with resources and Data. The Internet have Millions of users and is growing more and more every day. The Web contains Billions of Documents called Web Pages.

The Internet Web Page Link. ____

A Web Page on the Internet may link to other Web Documents, and to Text, Graphics, Sound and Video.

A Web site (Google) may contain a collection of related Web Pages. Computers store Web Pages

and the user, can use a Web Browser such as IE
(Internet Explorer) or Firefox to view them.

The content of those Web Pages can be:
Financial Data, News, Guides, Weather, Legal
Information, other..

A very important Web document or link is: "
The Future of Internet 2) a New Technology
and Standard for the Internet under
Development by the World Wide Web
Consortium (WWWC.) and/or W3C.

STOP WINDOWS 10 UPDATES FROM FORCING
UPDATES ON YOUR COMPUTER. ____

Option 1: Stop The Windows <u>Update Service</u>

As central as it is to the core of Windows 10, Windows Update is actually just another Windows process so it can be stopped with these simple steps:

> Open the Run command (Win + R), in it type: services.msc and press enter
> From the Services list which appears find the Windows Update service and open it
> In 'Startup Type' (under the 'General' tab) change it to 'Disabled'

> Restart

To re-enable Windows Update simply repeat these four steps, but change the Startup Type to 'Automatic'

OPTION 2:

Press the Windows logo key + R then type gpedit.msc and click OK. Go to Computer Configuration > Administrative Templates > Windows Components > Windows Update. Select <u>Disabled </u>in Configured Automatic Updates on the left, and click Apply and OK to disable the Windows automatic update feature.

Graphic Formats. _____

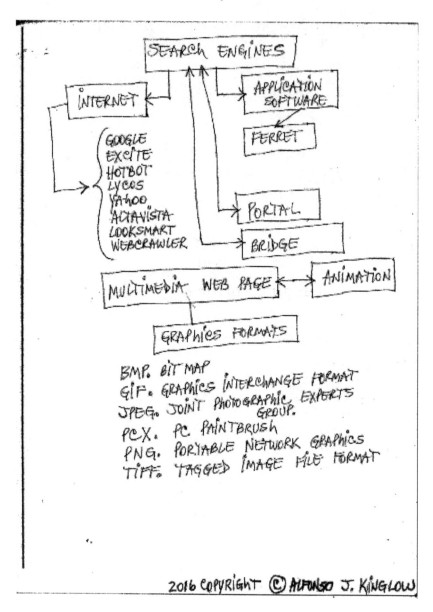

BMP. BIT MAP
GIF. GRAPHICS INTERCHANGE FORMAT
JPEG. JOINT PHOTOGRAPHIC EXPERTS GROUP.
PCX. PC PAINTBRUSH
PNG. PORTABLE NETWORK GRAPHICS
TIFF. TAGGED IMAGE FILE FORMAT

WINDOWS SECURITY. ___

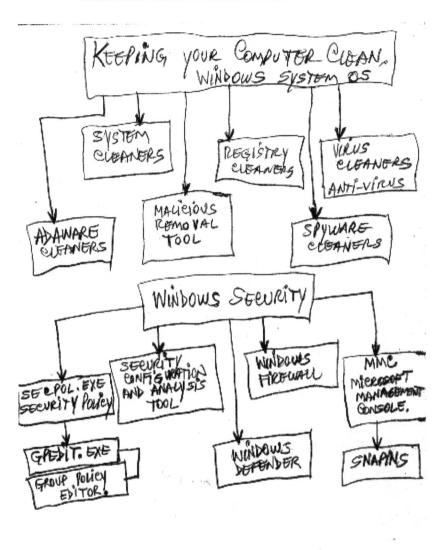

9 CHAPTER NINE

BASIC COMPUTER GLOSSARY. ___
The Beginning..

One of the earliest operating systems was **MS-DOS,** developed by Microsoft for IBM PC. It was a **Command Line Interface (CLI)** OS that revolutionized the PC market. **DOS** was difficult to use because of its interface. The users needed to remember instructions to do their tasks. To make computers more accessible and user-friendly, Microsoft developed **Graphical User Interface (GUI)** based OS called **Windows**, which transformed the way people used computers.

Basic Computer Glossary is different from **Basic Computer Terms.**

Applet

A small Java application that is downloaded by an ActiveX or Java-enabled web browser. Once it has been downloaded, the applet will run on the user's computer. Common applets include financial calculators and web drawing programs.

Application

Computer software that performs a task or set of tasks, such as word processing or drawing. Applications are also referred to as programs.

ASCII

American Standard Code for Information Interchange, an encoding system for converting keyboard characters and instructions into the binary number code that the computer understands.

Bandwidth

The capacity of a networked connection. Bandwidth determines how much data can be sent along the networked wires. Bandwidth is particularly important for Internet connections, since greater bandwidth also means faster downloads.

Binary code

The most basic language a computer understands, it is composed of a series of 0s and 1s. The computer interprets the code to form numbers, letters, punctuation marks, and symbols.

Bit

The smallest piece of computer information, either the number 0 or 1. In short they are called binary digits.

Boot

To start up a computer. Cold boot means restarting computer after the power is turned off. Warm boot means restarting computer without turning off the power.

Browser

Software used to navigate the Internet. Google Chrome, Firefox, Netscape Navigator and Microsoft Internet Explorer are today's most popular browsers for accessing the World Wide Web.

Bug

A malfunction due to an error in the program or a defect in the equipment.

Byte

Most computers use combinations of eight bits, called bytes, to represent one character of data or instructions. For example, the word **cat** has three characters, and it would be represented by three bytes.

Cache

A small data-memory storage area that a computer can use to instantly re-access data instead of re-

reading the data from the original source, such as a hard drive. Browsers use a cache to store web pages so that the user may view them again without reconnecting to the Web.

CAD-CAM

Computer Aided Drawing - Computer Aided Manufacturing. The instructions stored in a computer that will be translated to very precise operating instructions to a robot, such as for assembling cars or laser-cutting signage.

CD-ROM

Compact Disc Read-Only Memory, an optically read disc designed to hold information such as music, reference materials, or computer software. A single CD-ROM can hold around 640 megabytes of data, enough for several encyclopaedias. Most software programs are now delivered on CD-ROMs.

CGI

Common Gateway Interface, a programming standard that allows visitors to fill out form fields on a Web page and have that information interact with a database, possibly coming back to the user as another Web page. CGI may also refer to Computer-Generated Imaging, the process in which sophisticated computer programs create still and animated graphics, such as special effects for movies.

Chat

Typing text into a message box on a screen to engage in dialogue with one or more people via the Internet or other network.

Chip

A tiny wafer of silicon containing miniature electric circuits that can store millions of bits of information.

Client

A single user of a network application that is operated from a server. A client/server architecture allows many people to use the same data simultaneously. The program's main component (the data) resides on a centralized server, with smaller components (user interface) on each client.

Cookie

A text file sent by a Web server that is stored on the hard drive of a computer and relays back to the Web server things about the user, his or her computer, and/or his or her computer activities.

CPU

Central Processing Unit. The brain of the computer.

Cracker

A person who breaks in to a computer through a network, without authorization and with mischievous or destructive intent.

Crash

A hardware or software problem that causes information to be lost or the computer to malfunction. Sometimes a crash can cause permanent damage to a computer.

Cursor

A moving position-indicator displayed on a computer monitor that shows a computer operator where the next action or operation will take place.

Cyberspace

Slang for internet ie. An international conglomeration of interconnected computer networks. Begun in the late 1960s, it was developed in the 1970s to allow government and university researchers to share information. The Internet is not controlled by any single group or organization. Its original focus was research and communications, but it continues to expand, offering a wide array of resources for business and home users.

Database

A collection of similar information stored in a file, such as a database of addresses. This information may be created and stored in a database management system (DBMS).

Debug

Slang. To find and correct equipment defects or program malfunctions.

Default

The pre-defined configuration of a system or an application. In most programs, the defaults can be changed to reflect personal preferences.

Desktop

The main directory of the user interface. Desktops usually contain icons that represent links to the hard drive, a network (if there is one), and a trash or recycling can for files to be deleted. It can also display icons of frequently used applications, as requested by the user.

Desktop publishing

The production of publication-quality documents using a personal computer in combination with text, graphics, and page layout programs.

Directory

A repository where all files are kept on computer.

Disk

Two distinct types. The names refer to the media inside the container:

A hard disc stores vast amounts of data. It is usually inside the computer but can be a separate peripheral on the outside. Hard discs are made up of several rigid coated metal discs. Currently, hard discs can store 15 to 30 Gb (gigabytes).

A floppy disc, 3.5" square, usually inserted into the computer and can store about 1.4 megabytes of data. The 3.5" square floppies have a very thin, flexible disc inside. There is also an intermediate-sized floppy disc, trademarked Zip discs, which can store 250 megabytes of data.

Disk drive

The equipment that operates a hard or floppy disc.

Domain

Represents an IP (Internet Protocol) address or set of IP addresses that comprise a domain. The domain name appears in URLs to identify web pages or in email addresses. For example, the email address for the First Lady is first.lady@whitehouse.gov, whitehouse.gov, being the domain name. Each domain name ends with a suffix that indicates what top level domain it belongs to. These are : .com for commercial, .gov for government, .org for organization, .edu for educational institution, .biz for business, .info for information, .tv for television, .ws for website. Domain suffixes may also indicate the country in which the domain is registered. No two parties can ever hold the same domain name.

Domain name

The name of a network or computer linked to the Internet. Domains are defined by a common IP address or set of similar IP (Internet Protocol) addresses.

Download

The process of transferring information from a web site (or other remote location on a network) to the computer. It is possible to download a file which include text, image, audio, video and many others.

DOS

Disk Operating System. An operating system designed for early IBM-compatible PCs.

Drop-down menu

A menu window that opens vertically on-screen to display context-related options. Also called pop-up menu or pull-down menu.

DSL

Digital Subscriber Line, a method of connecting to the Internet via a phone line. A DSL connection uses copper telephone lines but is able to relay data at much higher speeds than modems and does not interfere with telephone use.

DVD

Digital Video Disc. Similar to a CD-ROM, it stores and plays both audio and video.

E-book

An electronic (usually hand-held) reading device that allows a person to view digitally stored reading materials.

Email

Electronic mail; messages, including memos or letters, sent electronically between networked computers that may be across the office or around the world.

Emoticon

A text-based expression of emotion created from ASCII characters that mimics a facial expression when viewed with your head tilted to the left. Here are some examples:

Smiling
Frowning
Winking

Crying

Encryption

The process of transmitting scrambled data so that only authorized recipients can unscramble it. For instance, encryption is used to scramble credit card information when purchases are made over the Internet.

Ethernet

A type of network.

Ethernet card

A board inside a computer to which a network cable can be attached.

File

A set of data that is stored in the computer.

Firewall

A set of security programs that protect a computer from outside interference or access via the Internet.

Folder

A structure for containing electronic files. In some operating systems, it is called a directory.

Fonts

Sets of typefaces (or characters) that come in different styles and sizes.

Freeware

Software created by people who are willing to give it away for the satisfaction of sharing or knowing they helped to simplify other people's lives. It may be free-standing software, or it may add functionality to existing software.

FTP

File Transfer Protocol, a format and set of rules for transferring files from a host to a remote computer.

Gigabyte (GB)

1024 megabytes. Also called gig.

Glitch

The cause of an unexpected malfunction.

Gopher

An Internet search tool that allows users to access textual information through a series of menus, or if using FTP, through downloads.

GUI

Graphical User Interface, a system that simplifies selecting computer commands by enabling the user to point to symbols or illustrations (called icons) on the computer screen with a mouse.

Groupware

Software that allows networked individuals to form groups and collaborate on documents, programs, or databases.

Hacker

A person with technical expertise who experiments with computer systems to determine how to develop additional features. Hackers are occasionally requested by system administrators to try and break into systems via a network to test security. The term hacker is sometimes incorrectly used interchangeably with cracker. A hacker is called a white hat and a cracker a black hat.

Hard copy

A paper printout of what you have prepared on the computer.

Hard drive

Another name for the hard disc that stores information in a computer.

Hardware

The physical and mechanical components of a computer system, such as the electronic circuitry, chips, monitor, disks, disk drives, keyboard, modem, and printer.

Home page

The main page of a Web site used to greet visitors, provide information about the site, or to direct the viewer to other pages on the site.

HTML

Hypertext Markup Language, a standard of text markup conventions used for documents on the World Wide Web. Browsers interpret the codes to give the text structure and formatting (such as bold, blue, or italic).

HTTP

Hypertext Transfer Protocol, a common system used to request and send HTML documents on the World Wide Web. It is the first portion of all URL addresses on the World Wide Web.

HTTPS

Hypertext Transfer Protocol Secure, often used in intracompany internet sites. Passwords are required to gain access.

Hyperlink

Text or an image that is connected by hypertext coding to a different location. By selecting the text or image with a mouse, the computer jumps to (or displays) the linked text.

Hypermedia

Integrates audio, graphics, and/or video through links embedded in the main program.

Hypertext

A system for organizing text through links, as opposed to a menu-driven hierarchy such as Gopher. Most Web pages include hypertext links to other pages at that site, or to other sites on the World Wide Web.

Icons

Symbols or illustrations appearing on the computer screen that indicate program files or other computer functions.

Input

Data that goes into a computer device.

Input device

A device, such as a keyboard, stylus and tablet, mouse, puck, or microphone, that allows input of information (letters, numbers, sound, video) to a computer.

Instant messaging (IM)

A chat application that allows two or more people to communicate over the Internet via real-time keyed-in messages.

Interface

The interconnections that allow a device, a program, or a person to interact. Hardware interfaces are the cables that connect the device to its power source and to other devices. Software interfaces allow the program to communicate with other programs (such as the operating system), and user interfaces allow the user to communicate with the program (e.g., via mouse, menu commands, icons, voice commands, etc.).

Internet

An international conglomeration of interconnected computer networks. Begun in the late 1960s, it was developed in the 1970s to allow government and university researchers to share information. The Internet is not controlled by any single group or organization. Its original focus was research and communications, but it continues to expand, offering a wide array of resources for business and home users.

IP (Internet Protocol) address

An Internet Protocol address is a unique set of numbers used to locate another computer on a network. The format of an IP address is a 32-bit string of four numbers separated by periods. Each number can be from 0 to 255 (i.e., 1.154.10.255). Within a closed network IP addresses may be assigned at random, however, IP addresses of web servers must be registered to avoid duplicates.

Java

An object-oriented programming language designed specifically for programs (particularly multimedia) to be used over the Internet. Java allows programmers to create small programs or applications (applets) to enhance Web sites.

JavaScript/ECMA script

A programming language used almost exclusively to manipulate content on a web page. Common JavaScript functions include validating forms on a web page, creating dynamic page navigation menus, and image rollovers.

Kilobyte (K or KB)

Equal to 1,024 bytes.

Linux

A UNIX - like, open-source operating system developed primarily by Linus Torvalds. Linux is free and runs on many platforms, including both PCs and Macintoshes. Linux is an open-source operating system, meaning that the source code of the operating system is freely available to the public. Programmers may redistribute and modify the code, as long as they don't collect royalties on their work or deny access to their code. Since development is not restricted to a single corporation more programmers can debug and improve the source code faster.

Laptop and notebook

Small, lightweight, portable battery-powered computers that can fit onto your lap. They each have a thin, flat, liquid crystal display screen.

Macro

A script that operates a series of commands to perform a function. It is set up to automate repetitive tasks.

Mac OS

An operating system with a graphical user interface, developed by Apple for Macintosh computers. Current System X.1.(10) combines the traditional Mac interface with a strong underlying UNIX. Operating system for increased performance and stability.

Megabyte (MB)

Equal to 1,048,576 bytes, usually rounded off to one million bytes (also called a meg).

Memory

Temporary storage for information, including applications and documents. The information must be stored to a permanent device, such as a hard disc or CD-ROM before the power is turned off, or the information will be lost. Computer memory is measured in terms of the amount of information it can store, commonly in megabytes or gigabytes.

Menu

A context-related list of options that users can choose from.

Menu bar

The horizontal strip across the top of an application's window. Each word on the strip has a context sensitive drop-down menu containing features and actions that are available for the application in use.

Merge

To combine two or more files into a single file.

MHz

An abbreviation for **Megahertz,** or **one million hertz.** One MHz represents one million clock cycles per second and is the measure of a computer microprocessor's speed. For example, a microprocessor that runs at 300 MHz executes 300 million cycles per second. Each instruction a computer receives takes a fixed number of clock cycles to carry out, therefore the more cycles a computer can execute per second, the faster its programs run. Megahertz is also a unit of measure for bandwidth.

Microprocessor

A complete central processing unit (CPU) contained on a single silicon chip.

Minimize

A term used in a GUI operating system that uses windows. It refers to reducing a window to an icon, or a label at the bottom of the screen, allowing another window to be viewed.

Modem

A device that connects two computers together over a telephone or cable line by converting the computer's data into an audio signal. Modem is a contraction for the process it performs : modulate-demodulate.

Monitor

A video display terminal.

Mouse

A small hand-held device, similar to a trackball, used to control the position of the cursor on the video display; movements of the mouse on a desktop correspond to movements of the cursor on the screen.

MP3

Compact audio and video file format. The small size of the files makes them easy to download and e-mail. Format used in portable playback devices.

Multimedia

Software programs that combine text and graphics with sound, video, and animation. A multimedia PC contains the hardware to support these capabilities.

MS-DOS

An early operating system developed by Microsoft Corporation (Microsoft Disc Operating System).

Network

A system of interconnected computers.

Open source

Computer programs whose original source code was revealed to the general public so that it could be developed openly. Software licensed as open source can be freely changed or adapted to new uses, meaning that the source code of the operating system is freely available to the public. Programmers may redistribute and modify the code, as long as they don't collect royalties on their work or deny access to their code. Since development is not restricted to a single corporation more programmers can debug and improve the source code faster.

Operating system

A set of instructions that tell a computer on how to operate when it is turned on. It sets up a filing system to store files and tells the computer how to display information on a video display. Most PC operating systems are DOS (disc operated system) systems, meaning the instructions are stored on a disc (as opposed to being originally stored in the microprocessors of the computer). Other well-known operating systems include UNIX, Linux, Macintosh, and Windows.

Output

Data that come out of a computer device. For example, information displayed on the monitor, sound from the speakers, and information printed to paper.

Palm

A hand-held computer.

PC

Personal computer. Generally refers to computers running Windows with a Pentium processor.

PC board

Printed Circuit board, a board printed or etched with a circuit and processors. Power supplies, information storage devices, or changers are attached.

PDA

Personal Digital Assistant, a hand-held computer that can store daily appointments, phone numbers, addresses, and other important information. Most PDAs link to a desktop or laptop computer to download or upload information.

PDF

Portable Document Format, a format presented by Adobe Acrobat that allows documents to be shared over a variety of operating systems. Documents can contain words and pictures and be formatted to have electronic links to other parts of the document or to places on the web.

Pentium chip

Intel's fifth generation of sophisticated high-speed microprocessors. Pentium means the fifth element.

Peripheral

Any external device attached to a computer to

enhance operation. Examples include external hard drive, scanner, printer, speakers, keyboard, mouse, trackball, stylus and tablet, and joystick.

Personal computer (PC)

A single-user computer containing a central processing unit (CPU) and one or more memory circuits.

Petabyte

A measure of memory or storage capacity and is approximately a thousand terabytes.

Petaflop

A theoretical measure of a computer's speed and can be expressed as a thousand-trillion floating-point operations per second.

Platform

The operating system, such as UNIX, Macintosh, Windows, on which a computer is based.

Plug and play

Computer hardware or peripherals that come set up with necessary software so that when attached to a computer, they are recognized by the computer and are ready to use.

Pop-up menu

A menu window that opens vertically or horizontally on-screen to display context-related options. Also called drop-down menu or pull-down menu.

Power PC

A competitor of the Pentium chip. It is a new generation of powerful sophisticated microprocessors produced from an Apple-IBM-Motorola alliance.

Printer

A mechanical device for printing a computer's output on paper. There are three major types of printer:

Dot matrix - creates individual letters, made up of a series of tiny ink dots, by punching a ribbon with the ends of tiny wires. (This type of printer is most often used in industrial settings, such as direct mail for labelling.)

Ink jet - sprays tiny droplets of ink particles onto paper.

Laser - uses a beam of light to reproduce the image of each page using a magnetic charge that attracts dry toner that is transferred to paper and sealed with heat.

Program

A precise series of instructions written in a computer language that tells the computer what to do and how to do it. Programs are also called software or applications.

Programming language

A series of instructions written by a programmer according to a given set of rules or conventions (syntax). High-level programming languages are independent of the device on which the application (or program) will eventually run; low-level languages are specific to each program or platform. Programming language instructions are converted into programs in language specific to a particular machine or operating system (machine language). So that the computer can interpret and carry out the instructions. Some common programming languages are BASIC, C, C++, dBASE, FORTRAN, and Perl.

Puck

An input device, like a mouse. It has a magnifying glass with crosshairs on the front of it that allows the operator to position it precisely when tracing a drawing for use with CAD-CAM software.

Pull-down menu

A menu window that opens vertically on-screen to

display context-related options. Also called drop-down menu or pop-up menu.

Push technology

Internet tool that delivers specific information directly to a user's desktop, eliminating the need to surf for it. PointCast, which delivers news in user-defined categories, is a popular example of this technology.

QuickTime

Audio-visual software that allows movie-delivery via the Internet and e-mail. QuickTime images are viewed on a monitor.

RAID

Redundant Array of Inexpensive Disks, a method of spreading information across several disks set up to act as a unit, using two different techniques:

10. **Disk striping -** storing a bit of information across several discs (instead of storing it all on one disc and hoping that the disc doesn't crash).

11. **Disk mirroring -** simultaneously storing a copy of information on another disc so that the information can be recovered if the main disc crashes.

RAM

Random Access Memory, one of two basic types of memory. Portions of programs are stored in RAM when the program is launched so that the program will run faster. Though a PC has a fixed amount of RAM, only portions of it will be accessed by the computer at any given time. Also called memory.

Right-click

Using the right mouse button to open context-sensitive drop-down menus.

ROM

Read-Only Memory, one of two basic types of memory. ROM contains only permanent information put there by the manufacturer. Information in ROM cannot be altered, nor can the memory be dynamically allocated by the computer or its operator.

Scanner

An electronic device that uses light-sensing equipment to scan paper images such as text, photos, and illustrations and translate the images into signals that the computer can then store, modify, or distribute.

Search engine

Software that makes it possible to look for and retrieve material on the Internet, particularly the Web. Some popular search engines are Alta Vista, Google, HotBot, Yahoo!, Web Crawler, and Lycos.

Server

A computer that shares its resources and information with other computers, called clients, on a network.

Shareware

Software created by people who are willing to sell it at low cost or no cost for the gratification of sharing. It may be freestanding software, or it may add functionality to existing software.

Software

Computer programs; also called applications.

Spider

A process search engines use to investigate new pages on a web site and collect the information that needs to be put in their indices.

Spreadsheet

Software that allows one to calculate numbers in a

format that is similar to pages in a conventional ledger.

Storage

Devices used to store massive amounts of information so that it can be readily retrieved. Devices include RAIDs, CD-ROMs, DVDs.

Streaming

Taking packets of information (sound or visual) from the Internet and storing it in temporary files to allow it to play in continuous flow.

Stylus and tablet

An input device similar to a mouse. The stylus is pen shaped. It is used to draw on a tablet (like drawing on paper) and the tablet transfers the information to the computer. The tablet responds to pressure. The firmer the pressure used to draw, the thicker the line appears.

Surfing

Exploring the Internet.

Surge protector

A controller to protect the computer and make up for variances in voltage.

Telnet

A way to communicate with a remote computer over a network.

Trackball

Input device that controls the position of the cursor on the screen; the unit is mounted near the keyboard, and movement is controlled by moving a ball.

Terabytes (TB)

A thousand gigabytes.

Teraflop

A measure of a computer's speed. It can be expressed as a trillion floating-point operations per second.

Trojan Horse

See virus.

UNIX

A very powerful operating system used as the basis of many high-end computer applications.

Upload

The process of transferring information from a

computer to a web site (or other remote location on a network). To transfer information from a computer to a web site (or other remote location on a network).

URL

Uniform Resource Locator.

The protocol for identifying a document on the Web.

A Web address (e.g., www.tutorialspoint.com). A URL is unique to each user. See also domain.

UPS

Universal Power Supply or Uninterruptible Power Supply. An electrical power supply that includes a battery to provide enough power to a computer during an outage to back-up data and properly shut down.

USB

A multiple-socket USB connector that allows several USB-compatible devices to be connected to a computer.

USENET

A large unmoderated and unedited bulletin board on the Internet that offers thousands of forums, called newsgroups. These range from newsgroups exchanging information on scientific advances to celebrity fan clubs.

User friendly

A program or device whose use is intuitive to people with a non-technical background.

Video teleconferencing

A remote "face-to-face chat," when two or more people using a webcam and an Internet telephone connection chat online. The webcam enables both live voice and video.

Virtual reality (VR)

A technology that allows one to experience and interact with images in a simulated three-dimensional environment. For example, you could design a room in a house on your computer and actually feel that you are walking around in it even though it was never built. (The Holodeck in the science-fiction TV series Star Trek : Voyager would be the ultimate virtual reality.) Current technology requires the user to wear a special helmet, viewing goggles, gloves, and other equipment that transmits and receives information from the computer.

Virus

An unauthorized piece of computer code attached

to a computer program or portions of a computer system that secretly copies itself from one computer to another by shared discs and over telephone and cable lines. It can destroy information stored on the computer, and in extreme cases, can destroy operability. Computers can be protected from viruses if the operator utilizes good virus prevention software and keeps the virus definitions up to date. Most viruses are not programmed to spread themselves. They have to be sent to another computer by e-mail, sharing, or applications. The worm is an exception, because it is programmed to replicate itself by sending copies to other computers listed in the e-mail address book in the computer. There are many kinds of viruses, for example:

Boot viruses place some of their code in the start-up disk sector to automatically execute when booting. Therefore, when an infected machine boots, the virus loads and runs.

File viruses attached to program files (files with the extension .exe). When you run the infected program, the virus code executes.

Macro viruses copy their macros to templates and/or other application document files.

Trojan Horse is a malicious, security-breaking program that is disguised as something being such as a screen saver or game.

Worm launches an application that destroys information on your hard drive. It also sends a copy of the virus to everyone in the computer's e-mail address book.

WAV

A sound format (pronounced wave) used to reproduce sounds on a computer.

Webcam

A video camera/computer setup that takes live images and sends them to a Web browser.

Window

A portion of a computer display used in a graphical interface that enables users to select commands by pointing to illustrations or symbols with a mouse. "Windows" is also the name Microsoft adopted for its popular operating system.

World Wide Web ("WWW" or "the Web")

A network of servers on the Internet that use hypertext-linked databases and files. It was developed in 1989 by Tim Berners-Lee, a British computer scientist, and is now the primary platform of the Internet. The feature that distinguishes the Web from other Internet applications is its ability to display graphics in addition to text.

Word processor

A computer system or program for setting, editing, revising, correcting, storing, and printing text.

WYSIWYG

What You See Is What You Get. When using most word processors, page layout programs (See desktop publishing), and web page design programs, words and images will be displayed on the monitor as they will look on the printed page or web page.

COMPUTER TERMS

Basic Computer Terms

Bit - A binary unit of data storage that can only be a value of 0 or 1.

BIOS - BIOS stands for Basic Input/Output System and it is a low level program used by your system to interface to computer devices such as your video card, keyboard, mouse, hard drive, and other devices.

Boot - A term used to describe what happens to a computer when it is turned on, the operating system begins to run, and then the user is able to use the computer successfully.

Byte - 8 bits of data which has a possible value from 0 to 255.

CD-ROM disk - A disk with about 640Mb of storage capacity which are more commonly read than written to.

CD-ROM drive - The hardware component that is used to read a CD-ROM or write to it.

Crash - A common term used to describe what happens to a computer when software errors force it to quit operating and become unresponsive to a computer user.

Driver - A specially written program which

understands the operation of the device it interfaces to, such as a printer, video card, sound card or CD ROM drive. It provides an interface for the operating system to use the device.

File - A collection of data into a permanent storage structure. Stored on a permanent storage media such as a computer hard drive.

Firmware - Software written into permanent storage into the computer.

Floppy disk - A low capacity storage media which can be written to as easily as it is read.

Floppy Drive - The hardware component that is used to read or write to a floppy disk.

Hardware - Describes the physical parts of your computer which you can physically touch or see such as your monitor, case, disk drives, microprocessor and other physical parts.

Internet - A network of networks which incorporate a many organizations, physical lines, the ability to route data, and many services including email and web browsing.

ISP - Internet Service Provider is an organization that provides the ability to connect to the internet for their customers. They also usually provide additional services such as e-mail and the ability to host web sites.

MIME - multipurpose internet mail extension

Memory - Used to provide the temporary storage of information function.

Network - A general term describing to the cables and electronic components that carry data between computers. It is also generally used to refer to the server computers that provide services such as printing, file sharing, e-mail, and other services.

Operating System - The core software component of a computer providing the ability to interface to peripheral and external devices along with program functions to support application programs.

Parallel - A data transmission method where data is sent on more than one line at a time. This may be any number of bits at a time, but is usually one word at a time (two bytes) or possibly three bytes at a time.

Protocols - A standard method used for communications or other internet and network functions.

Security flaw - A software bug allowing an attacker a method to gain unauthorized access to a system.

Serial - A data transmission method where data is sent on a single line and one bit is sent at at a time. This is similar to a line which one item must come one after another

Software - Describes the programs that run on your system.

SPAM - A term used to describe junk and unsolicited e-mail.

Storage Media - A term used to describe any magnetic device that computer data can be permanently stored on such as a hard drive or floppy drive.

URL - Uniform Resource Locator is the term used to describe a link which points to a location of a file on the internet.

Virus - A program that runs on a system against the owner's or user's wishes and knowledge and can spread by infecting files or sending itself through e-mail

Vulnerability - Software errors that allow some kind of unauthorized access when they are used or exploited.

Word - Two bytes or 16 bits of data with a possible unsigned value from 0 to 16535.

Worm - A term used to describe an unwanted program that uses system or application vulnerabilities to infect a computer without the user doing anything but connecting to an infected network.

10 CHAPTER TEN

NEW WI -FI STANDARD. ____

From Huawei. Internet Source.

The New Wi-Fi Standard That Will Make the 802.11AC Obsolete.__

The first wave of 802.11ac routers currently available on the market are based on earlier drafts of the 802.11ac standard and will no longer be the fastest standard on the market. The second wave of 802.11ac devices are based on the final ratified standard and are set to include new features that better optimize wireless networks.

802.11AC Standard: Wave 1 vs. Wave 2

802.11ac Wave 2 is set to include MU-MIMO capabilities among other advances that will give routers a speed boost from the original 3.47 Gbps in first generation to 6.93 Gbps in the final iteration of the standard.

MU-MIMO or Multiple-user multiple input/multiple output "enables [routers] to send multiple spatial streams to multiple clients

simultaneously". With 160 MHz channel bonding (as

opposed to 80 Mhz bonding over wave 1) and

backwards compatibility with previous standards, the new standard boasts a performance boost over the first generation of 802.11ac routers. With a physical link rate of nearly 7 Gbps, users hoping to upgrade to 802.11ac <u>should consider waiting to catch the second wave.</u>

Market Trends

Dell'Oro Group has published a report that notes that the "Wireless LAN (WLAN) market grew eight percent in the third quarter 2014 versus the year-ago period" and that "Enterprise-class 802.11ac-based radio access points grew a robust 40 percent versus the second quarter 2014."

The report forecasts that the WLAN market will be stimulated with the release of 802.11ac Wave 2 equipment along with government funding in the US meant to support wireless connectivity in schools and libraries.

The New Standard 802.11ax

But even the second generation of the 802.11ac standard cannot compare with the wireless speeds of a still newer specification. The 802.11ax standard is set to "not just increase the overall speed of a network"but to "quadruple wireless speeds of

individual clients." Huawei's research and development labs , have reported to successfully reach wireless connections speeds of 10 Gbps utilizing the 5GHz frequency band.

The standard is set to be finalized in 2019, but manufacturers can be expected to release products based on the pre-standard as early as 2018.

While wireless connections keep getting faster, the options for internet users to connect to the internet keep expanding. In the near future, users can be expected to connect to the internet using LED lights, or gain wireless access to the internet by connecting to a micro-satellite orbiting the Earth.

Networx™ USB 3.0 SuperSpeed Cables combine style, quality, performance and value to give a great deal on a great USB cable. The molded connectors are designed to make them easy to grip. Networx™ USB 3.0 cables are double-shielded with a dual foil and braid. The connector is surrounded by a metal shield and the cable braid is also soldered to the connector to create an end-to-end full shielding solution guaranteeing a noise-free connection. SuperSpeed USB 3.0 is 2nd revision of the ubiquitous USB (Universal Serial Bus) Standard. Clocking in at speeds up to 5 Gbit/s, USB 3.0 is a vast improvement over the USB 2.0 speed of 400 Mbit/s while being completely backwards compatible with USB 2.0.

USB 3.0 A Male to A Female

Up to 5Gbit/sec

PC and Mac Compatible

Ultra-flexible jacket; Molded strain relief

Foil and braid shield to guarantee an interference free connection

Proper current to your USB device via Heavy-duty 24AWG power wire

EMI/RFI int: Metal connector shield to meet FCC requirements

USB 3.0 and 3.1 New Cable Standard. __

Source: Public Domain/Open Source

USB 3.0 REGISTERED SEAL AND LOGO.____

USB 3.0 is the third major version of the Universal Serial Bus standard for interfacing computers and electronic devices. Among other improvements, USB 3.0 adds the new transfer rate referred to as SuperSpeed USB that can transfer data at up to 5 Gbit/s, which is about 10 times as fast as the USB 2.0 standard.

Manufacturers are recommended to distinguish USB 3.0 connectors from their USB 2.0 counterparts by blue color-coding of the Standard-A receptacles and plugs, and by the initials SS.

11 CHAPTER ELEVEN

BASIC INFORMATION ABOUT HARDWARE.__

The Hardware is the box or frame that contains all the major parts of a computer, the internal hard drive, the CD/DVD Player, the different input ports, the keyboard and mouse, the processor and ram memory, the Ethernet network card, the Wireless network card, the video display, the LCD display(on laptops), the sound card, the internal built in camera, the internal microphone, etc.. One of the major Ports is the USB (Universal Serial Bus) that is now used to connect Printers, Cameras and multiple other devices to your computer hardware.

Policies are built into the computer hardware to allow for security and to manage the hardware. Some of the most important policies are the SECPOL. MSC (Security Policy) and GPEDIT. MSC (Group Policy Editor) these policies allow you to setup the security configuration on your computer hardware. These policies are launched using the Command Line (CMD) built into your computer, or by typing the policy directly into the START or RUN line. The Command Line CMD is provided as a means of accessing your Computer Hardware and Software policies and to directly manage a great part of your computer hardware, without requiring any software to manage policies.

It is used also for direct maintenance of the computer and comes with a reasonable help file. This file contains all of the commands used with the CMD. The command line window when launched appears with a black background. The background and text colors can be changed from a menu of different colors as well as the text size and window size. Some preferred combinations are; red background with yellow text color or green background with white or purple text color, etc... To change the color background and text, click on the CMD icon in the upper left side of the command window.

To access all of the standard policies to set up your computer hardware you can find them in the MMC (Microsoft Management Console) built into your computer hardware.

The MMC allow the user to create Snap-in's to setup the hardware and security configuration. To access the MMC just type it into the CMD window or directly into the START or RUN line, on the lower left side of your computer.

A View of Computer Configuration with Applications and Utilities. ____

The User Tools and System Tools are presented in a Graphic configuration easy to understand. All the

Diagnostic Tools that are built-into Windows are shown and are available to the user, for diagnostics and troubleshooting the computer.

Twelve Diagnostic Tools are shown that are built into Windows. All these tools can be access by the user. If the Computer is running Windows 10, just type in the name of the tool in Cortana, to access, or just type the name into the Start area for all other Systems.

MORE PERFORMANCE FROM WINDOWS OS.

To get more Performance from Windows OS, open the Taskbar and type: **sysdm.cpl** into the search box.

Next press <Enter>

Switch to the Advanced Tab, under the Performance, click the Settings button to disable Windows Animations, Fades, Font smoothing, drop shadows behind dialog boxes, and other visual enhancements that take up more memory and processor time.

To keep Windows as visually back as possible, click the "Adjust for Best Performance" Checkbox; Exit and Restart.

12 CHAPTER TWELVE
SOFTWARE.

BASIC INFORMATION ABOUT SOFTWARE. __

Software are the Programs that make all of the Hardware work. The major software in any computer system will be the OS or Operating System such as Windows. The other major software will be the Applications and Utilities. Some software will need to be installed by the user and some will be installed by the OS or Operating System. Major user software will be the Applications such as Microsoft Office, and others that will facilitate the users to become more productive. Utilities will protect the computer from threats and viruses.

Software programs in general are divided into the following areas: Software Applications, Productivity, Games, Development, Multimedia, Educational, Utilities, System, LAN Local Area Networks, Web Software, Maintenance, Network, Paint, Accessories, Programming, Basic, Communications, Cloud Software, WAN Wide Area Network (The Internet), Graphics, Antivirus, etc...

Software programs are Installed, Deleted, Removed, and Purged.

When a Software program is Installed, it must be Un-Installed.

When a software program is Deleted, it must be Un-Deleted.

To correctly remove Software Programs, it must be done in the Control Panel in Programs and Features, if you are running Windows 8. The program is then Uninstalled or Changed.

Dragging a program to the Trash or Recycle Bin does not Remove it, to Remove a program it must be Shredded in the Recycle Bin.

To Destroy a program it must be Purged.

Most Software are in the following modes, Virtual Software, Hyper-V Software, Free Software, Search Software, Shared Software, Open Source Software, Public Domain Software, License Software, Encrypted Software, Decrypted Software, Cipher Software, Network Card Test Software or (loop back address Software), OS Windows Software(Operating Systems); Firewall Software, Security Software(Bit Locker), Printer Software, Email Software, DSL Router Software, etc..

Software Languages and Standards. __

Most Software are written in the following computer languages: Hypertext, used in Web Browsers on the Internet, Unix, Basic, Ada, C and C++ (C Plus Plus), Html (Hypertext Markup Language), Xml   (Extensible Markup Language), Fortran, Pascal, and High Level Compilers, etc....

The Standards that govern Software are: Defacto Standards, IEEE Project 802.x, The OSI Model and the ISO (International Standards Organization).

The Seven Pillars to Execute Software Programs.__

Setup and Install the Software

Uninstall and Undelete

Add and Remove

User Install and System Install

Run, Search and Delete

Free, Trial and Test

Open Source and Public Domain software access

Search Software Formats. __

The following Search Software Formats are used on the Internet as follows:

Search with --------☐ AND or + ------☐ Red Cars and Red Vans.   Green Apples + Red Apples.

Search with -------☐ OR ---------☐ One word to be in search   (Flight Attendant Stewardess.)

Search with ------☐ AND NOT (-) -☐ suv AND

NOT auto   (suv – auto)

Search with ----☐ Phrase Searching --☐ Exact Phrase within   " Harry Potter"   Quotation.

Search with ----□ Wildcard ---□ WRIT* CLOU* -□ The Asterisk at the end of words.

Semantic Search Engines on the Internet.__

1. DuckDuckGo

2. Dogpile

3. WebCrawler

4. Ask.com

5. Hakia.com

6. Momma.com

Semantic Search and the Semantic Web.__

While *Semantic Web* and *Semantic Search* are not the same thing, the two concepts are often confused.

The fact that these two families of technologies share the word *semantic* has led to some confusion

about the difference between them. According to Merriam-Webster, semantic means "of or related to meaning." Both of these kinds of technologies attempt to retrieve and present information based on its meaning rather than on its structure or intended usage, as more traditional technologies do. Although they are related, the two technologies in fact solve different problems.

In brief, **Semantic Search** is useful for searching on a single type of data in a single domain, whereas **Semantic Web** technologies are useful for querying <u>across many types of related information</u>. Consider a few examples of each kind of technology.

Although Google generally does a good job in ranking web pages, most of us know that this kind of search completely fails in other contexts. For example, searching your own computer for a document by relying on keywords can be very frustrating—not to mention searching a data store the size of your corporate intranet! In such cases, you will not succeed unless you know exactly what you are looking for. This shortfall is not the fault of the technology itself;

This is where Semantic Search comes in. Rather than blindly returning anything that contains the text you typed into the search bar, Semantic Search takes into account **the *context* of your search** <u>as well as</u> **the underlying meaning of the documents to be searched.**

However, what if you were searching for *jaguar*, the predatory black feline? Or *Jaguar*, the Mac 10.2 operating system? Or *Jaguar*, the Atari system? Even on Google, straightforward keyword searching <u>does not take into account the context of your search, nor does it understand the meaning of the documents.</u>

In an attempt to do a better job, Semantic Search technologies employ various methods (NLP, statistical modeling, etc.), to categorize and/or cluster related documents to ease searching.

Semantic Web._____

The Semantic Web is a set of technologies for representing, storing, and querying information. Although these technologies *can* be used to store textual data—such as text in a Word document or PDF file—they typically are used to store smaller bits of data. Thus, while Semantic Search focuses largely on textual information, **the Semantic Web** <u>also includes numbers, dates, figures, and other data in addition to text.</u>

Semantic Web and Semantic Search Combined

Generally speaking, anything that can be accomplished with Semantic Search can be represented as a Semantic Web query. That is, Semantic Web technologies are sufficiently broad to encompass all Semantic Search capabilities.

A simple way to think about which family of technologies might be useful for a specific problem is to ask yourself whether your users are searching on only one kind of information (e.g., restaurants, a flight number, etc.), or whether they are searching on many kinds of information (e.g., which presidents had children who did not live in the White House).

Semantic Web vendors focus on solving problems using many different kinds of information. Instead of simply storing data about restaurants, a Semantic Web application would have access to information about the chefs, the cities, the menus, the cuisine styles, the décor, the wine list, the wineries that produced the wine on the wine list, etc.

However, if you need to answer a question such as, **"What restaurants in Boston have several wines that were produced in the Alsace region between 1998 and 2001?"** then Semantic Search will not be able to help you; instead, you will need the **Semantic Web**.

Setup Windows Power Option in the Control Panel.

Goto the **Control Panel** in Windows, open the Power Options App

Setup each of the Power Options, they must be set to **Never, Never, Never** and **Do Nothing,** example like" When I close the lid"; Do Nothing..etc..

ANTIVIRUS to keep your Computer Clean. __

To Protect your Computer from Viruses, you will need an ANTI-VIRUS Program or Application Installed directly on your Computer Hardware.

The Antivirus Application **AVG** is **Free** and can be downloaded from the Internet.

AVG have a Paid and a Free version; make sure you download the version that say; " FREE ".
When AVG is installed; run the program immediately.

Your Computer must be connected to the Internet the first time you run the program so that it can Update its VIRUS DEFINITION FILE.

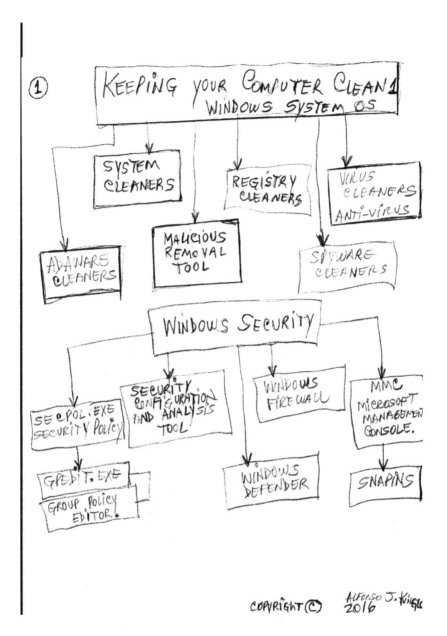

① KEEPING your COMPUTER CLEAN
WINDOWS SYSTEM OS

SYSTEM CLEANERS

REGISTRY CLEANERS

VIRUS CLEANERS ANTI-VIRUS

ADAWARE CLEANERS

MALICIOUS REMOVAL TOOL

SPYWARE CLEANERS

WINDOWS SECURITY

SECPOL.EXE SECURITY POLICY

SECURITY CONFIGURATION AND ANALYSIS TOOL

WINDOWS FIREWALL

MMC MICROSOFT MANAGEMEN CONSOLE.

GPEDIT.EXE GROUP POLICY EDITOR.

WINDOWS DEFENDER

SNAPINS

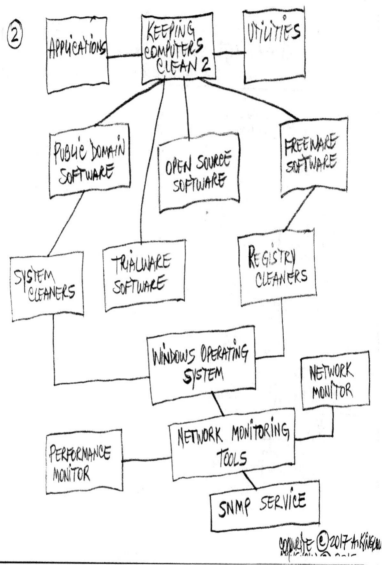

To find applications and utilities to keep your computer clean, go to the Internet Public Domain Software Area or the Open Source, or Freeware Areas on the Internet to find all kinds of FREE Software.

THE COMPUTER DESKTOP. ___

THE DESKTOP IS THE AREA THAT APPEARS RIGHT AFTER LOGGIN IN. IT CONTAINS A BACKGROUND PICTURE CALLED WALLPAPER, ICONS, AND THE TASKBAR.

THE PICTURES WITH THE TEXT LABELS UNDER THEM ARE CALLED ICONS, AND THEY REPRESENT THE SOFTWARE THEY ARE REPRESENTING. THEY USUALLY REPRESENT PROGRAMS BUT SOMETIMES THEY REPRESENT COLLECTIONS OF DATA. THE ICONS WILL OPEN WHATEVER IT REPRESENTS. THE TEXT TELLS WHAT IT REPRESENTS.

ICONS, ARE A TINY PICTURE THAT REPRESENTS A PROGRAM, FOLDER OR FUNCTION.

THE TASKBAR. __

THE TASKBAR
IS THE BAR THAT IS
AT THE BOTTOM OF THE
DESKTOP.
IT IS USED TO LAUNCH
PROGRAMS OR TO OPEN THE
WINDOW OF AN OPEN PROGRAM

THE BUTTON ON THE LEFT SIDE OF
THE START BAR IS CALLED THE START
BUTTON. WHEN YOU CLICK THE BUTTON
IT OPENS THE START MENU.

THE START-MENU HAS ICONS FOR MORE
PROGRAMS. AND DATA COLLECTIONS., IT
CONTAINS ICONS FOR ALL INSTALLED
PROGRAMS AND DATA COLLECTIONS.
THE ICONS ON THE DESKTOP, THE LAUNCH
BAR, AND THE START MENU ARE
SHORTCUTS.

TO KEEP YOUR COMPUTER CLEAN AND ENHANCE PERFORMANCE AND ELIMINATE MALWARE, ADAWARE AND SPYWARE. ___

Download the following Utilities and RUN them at least Once a Week or every two weeks.

Advanced System Care 12.1

Glary Utility 5.100

Clean Master 6.0

Acebyte Utility 3.2

BASIC INFORMATION ABOUT WINDOWS TOOLS.

Windows User Tools

Command prompt

Control Panel

Resource Monitor

Run Command

Slide to Shutdown

System Information

Task Manager

Safe Mode Shift + F8

 Special Menu Windows Key + "X" Key

Shell

Windows Diagnostic Tools:

MSConfig from RUN

3D Builder

Narrator

Performance monitor

Resource Monitor

RUN Command

System Configuration

Task Manager

Windows System Tools:

1. On Screen Keyboard

2. Phone companion

3. Phone

4. System Information

5. Uninstall

6. Windows memory Diagnostic

7. Win Patrol Explorer

8. Win Patrol Help

9. CMD Command Line

Windows Administrative Tools

Computer Management

Defragment drives

Disk Cleanup

Event Viewer

ISCSI Initiator

Local Security Policy

 ODBC Data Sources

Performance Monitor

Print Management

Recovery Drive

Resource Monitor

Services

System Configuration

System Information

Task Scheduler

Windows defender Firewall

Windows Memory Diagnostic

 Get more Performance from Windows with
sysdm.cpl

using RUN. Goto Settings in Performance tab.

ABOUT THE AUTHOR
Dr Alfonso J. Kinglow PhD

Professor Alfonso J. Kinglow have been teaching Computers, Networking and Science and Technology for many years. As an Adjunct Faculty member of NMSU New Mexico State University, in Las Cruces he started Computer classes for Seniors and beginners for several years at Munson Senior Center, in Las Cruces, and presently at Shadow Mountain Senior Center, in Phoenix, Arizona where he serves as a Volunteer. His classes are very successful and are always full. This Book shares Professor Kinglow vision in bringing modern Technology to all Users as well as Seniors and Beginners trying to keep up with Technology, in a very basic and comprehensive format that is easy to understand. It contains Graphic figures in a box format that makes it easy to convey the information, not just in text mode. The book contains all the built-in System Tools, and some hidden System and User Tools to empower the users to better understand their Computer Hardware and Software, and to be able to Maintain and Setup their own Computers and Security. With information on the new WI-Fi standard and updated system information.

Professor Kinglow received his PhD and many other

Awards and is the author of many technical innovations published by NASA. He received the October 2013 Volunteer Spotlight Award from The City of Las Cruces, and is featured in "Las Cruces Magazine" published by real View publishing, Las Cruces NM.

Dr. Kinglow have taught overseas at various Universities as a bilingual visiting Professor, and is a Systems Engineer by trade. While working for NASA he received the NASA STS-34 Award for outstanding dedication and Mission Support for the Galileo Mission.

Dr. Kinglow received many Commendations and Honors from NASA and Lockheed Engineering and Sciences Company, for his support of the Shuttle Missions., and is a member of The Computer Society.

THE AUTHOR

Dr Alfonso J. Kinglow PhD

The Author at Work.

Classes to Seniors.

Classes to Seniors

ALFONSO J. KINGLOW